RESTORING *the* PRIDE

PENN STATE'S 2005 CHAMPIONSHIP SEASON

SPORTS
PUBLISHING
L.L.C.

www.SportsPublishingLLC.com

www.SportsPublishingLLC.com

CENTRE DAILY TIMES
www.centredaily.com

Peter L. Bannon publisher

Joseph J. Bannon Sr. publisher

Susan M. Moyer senior managing editor

Noah Adams Amstadter acquisitions editor

Elisa Bock Laird developmental editor

K. Jeffrey Higgerson art director

Dustin Hubbart cover design, imaging

Kathryn R. Holleman interior layout

Erin Linden-Levy photo editor

Adrian Pratt publisher

Robert Heisse executive editor

Ron Bracken sports editor

Laurie Jones photo editor

Walt Moody assistant sports editor

Jeff Rice, Adam Gearhart,

Todd Ceisner, Gordon Brunskill,

Cecily Cairns sports staff

Craig Houtz, Michelle Klein,

Nabil K. Mark photography staff

ISBN: 1-59670-052-1
© 2005 Centre Daily Times

Front cover photo by
Ned Dishman/Getty Images
Back cover photo by
Craig Houtz/Centre Daily Times

Printed in the United States of America

Sports Publishing L.L.C.
804 North Neil Street • Champaign, IL 61820
Phone: 1-877-424-2665 • Fax: 217-363-2073
www.SportsPublishingLLC.com

All rights reserved. Except for use in a review, the reproduction or utilization of this work in any form or by any electronic, mechanical, or other means, now known or hereafter invented, including xerography, photocopying, and recording, and in any information storage and retrieval system, is forbidden without the written permission of the publisher.

CONTENTS

EDITOR'S NOTE

BY RON BRACKEN

Who knew?

Who could possibly have known that it would end like this?

Oh, there were a few loyalists who always believe Penn State is going to go 11-0 or 10-1. What team doesn't have a few of those at the core of its fan base?

But based on recent past performance and present players, most were prepared for Penn State to finish in the black numbers, but not by much. 7-4 or 6-5 were the most common predictions among the preseason pollsters.

And that would have been all right, given where the program had been in the past two years. Hey, it was a winning season, right? And it would have been a step back toward the upper echelon of the Big Ten.

No one could have predicted that this team would take such a giant leap, going from worst to first.

Well, almost no one. Joe Paterno, drawing from his 50-year database of experience, had a suspicion this team might be better than outsiders thought.

"I never thought we were that far away," he said frequently during the course of this magical season. "We just needed a couple of people to make a play."

The problem was, he didn't have them last year. This year he did. And it didn't matter that they were fuzzy-cheeked freshman wide receivers. They were playmakers, even if they only had to shave once every four days. As long as they kept their helmets on in the end zone, who knew if they had a five o'clock shadow?

They gave Michael Robinson reliable targets, spread defenses so tailback Tony Hunt could run and gave a rugged veteran defense time to catch its breath on the sidelines.

So while the postseason honors go to Robinson, to linebacker Paul Posluszny, defensive end Tamba Hali or cornerback Alan Zemaitis, no small measure of credit for this turnaround has to be laid at the feet of the freshmen—Derrick Williams, Justin King, Deon Butler and Jordan Norwood.

And a large portion must be accorded to Paterno, who never lost faith in his team, who wisely adjusted his offense to the skills of the players he brought in and the ones who had stayed with the program during the bad times.

Moreover, he delegated more of the coaching work to his assistants, allowing Galen Hall the freedom to run the offense and Tom Bradley the leeway to come up with a defensive package.

In the end, it all worked. And while he stopped just short of saying, "I told you so," to his doubters, Paterno knew it all along.

ABOVE: Penn State football captains Paul Posluszny (31), Michael Robinson (12), and Alan Zemaitis (21) have led the team and helped establish a successful atmosphere on and off the field.
Nabil K. Mark/Centre Daily Times

Senior defensive end Matthew Rice (55) and senior quarterback Michael Robinson (12) hug after leading Penn State to victory over Michigan State. The win cemented Penn State's right to a Bowl Championship Series bid and a share of the Big Ten title. *Craig Houtz/Centre Daily Times*

HEADACHES DO NOT HELP PSU'S RECOVERY

BY JEFF RICE

F or most of the spring and summer, tempered optimism flowed slowly through Nittany Nation. There were good reasons to believe that 2005 was not going to be a painful reprisal of Penn State's previous two seasons.

Favorable schedule? Check.

Loaded defense? Check.

Freakishly talented freshman receivers? Check.

Then the Nittany Lions started practice, and the dark cloud that has followed this program around suddenly returned. Telephone indiscretions, academic failures and a good ol' fashioned football injury were sharp slaps in the face to fans dreaming of a warm New Year's Day bowl venue.

The losses of Mark Rubin, Lavon Chisley and Dan Connor will hurt Penn State to varying degrees. Respectively, they rob experience from a receiving corps that had little to begin with; rob depth from a defensive line that didn't have that in stores; and temporarily halt what many believed to be the rise of the next great linebacker duo at Linebacker U.

On its own, each loss is negligible. But when a team is 7-16 over the last two seasons, the preseason

RIGHT: **Blue team's Tony Hunt powers his way past white team's Paul Cronin.**
Craig Houtz/Centre Daily Times

must be a time for stepping forward, not backward or even walking in place. The Nittany Lions are not in a position to shoot themselves in the feet; there are plenty of teams in the Big Ten waiting to do that for them.

The thing is, there are many reasons for optimism, including those mentioned above and a few others, like tailbacks Tony Hunt and Austin Scott, defensive ends Tamba Hali and Matt Rice as well as captains who can lead and play in Michael Robinson, Alan Zemaitis and Paul Posluszny.

It becomes harder and harder to surrender to that optimism, though, when the Nittany Lions prove time and again they're still a mess off the field. It does little good to blame the coaches or the captains, who have done nothing but dispense swift and fair punishment in front of (and no doubt behind) the curtain.

It does even less good to blame the media (stay with me here) for overplaying or downplaying incidents like the prank calls or "Arrowgate." The impact their stories have on the public has little effect on the impact the incidents themselves have on the team.

And that impact should not be dismissed. It is no coincidence that the Nittany Lions started their worst back-to-back seasons of football during the same year in which they had more publicized off-field indiscretions (some 11 in 12 months) than any in anyone's recent memory.

How much Penn State's image has been tarnished by wayward arrows, underage drinking charges or idiotic phone calls is up for debate, and it's not the real issue. The real issue is what it has done to the on-field makeup of a team that has struggled to put it together.

Chisley isn't the first Nittany Lion to be ruled academically ineligible and won't be the last, but suddenly Penn State's three-headed monster at defensive end is down to two heads. Maybe Josh Gaines is the future, but if he isn't, it could be a long season for Hali and Rice.

Penn State is deeper at linebacker than at any other position, but the loss of Connor nonetheless weakens a unit that will be called upon to help out a young defensive line, one that has a senior tackle (Scott Paxson) who is currently on the third team because of off-field mistakes.

Speaking of Arrowgate, on paper, the Nittany Lions could have lined up four seniors along the offensive line this fall. That would have been their most seasoned unit since 2002, when Penn State averaged 423.7 yards of offense per game. But E.Z. Smith messed up and, by not immediately coming clean, so did Tyler Reed and Andrew Richardson.

Maybe younger players making the most of the current situation, like Greg Harrison, A.Q. Shipley and Gerald Cadogan, would have unseated the upperclassmen anyway, but we'll never know.

Which is really the fear—that the Nittany Lions will continue to stumble enough off the field to keep them from reaching their full potential on it. The talent is there, the schedule is there. The coaches are all back, Paterno looks refreshed, Nittany Nation is ready to roar again.

Provided its team makes it through the rest of the preseason.

OPPOSITE PAGE: **Blue team's Derrick Williams scrambles after taking a snap from the center.**
Craig Houtz/Centre Daily Times

BULLISH BEGINNING

BY JEFF RICE

The yards on the stat sheet and the perpetual grin on Michael Robinson's face conveyed the sort of feeling Penn State had been hoping would follow its long-awaited season-opener.

How the Nittany Lions earned those yards and the fresh, two-stitch cut above Robinson's right eye told a much different tale.

On a picturesque September afternoon in Beaver Stadium, Penn State showed off its new offensive weapons and its old monster defense but, like the announced crowd of 99,235, knew its 23-13 defeat of South Florida wasn't nearly as easy as it could have been.

"It was a struggle for us," Robinson said. "Every special teams, offense and defense had to stick it in there and fight."

In his debut as the full-time starter at quarterback, Robinson endured many of those struggles as Penn State (1-0) broke in a retooled offensive line and brand-new receiving corps. The fifth-year senior was 9 of 15 for 90 yards and one interception, ran for 39 yards on 18 carries and scored Penn State's final touchdown on a four-yard

RIGHT: After snatching an interception, Penn State's Chris Harrell makes a break for the South Florida 12-yard line. *Craig Houtz/Centre Daily Times*

14

ABOVE: **Penn State's Alan Zemaitis returns a fumble for a score while being chased by USF's Amarri Jackson.**
Nabil K. Mark/Centre Daily Times

run four minutes into the fourth quarter. He also was sacked three times and lost two fumbles.

"I think we definitely have some things to work on," Robinson said. "There were some first-game jitters for a lot of people out there, myself included."

The Nittany Lions defense, which finished 10th in the nation in total defense last season, did not allow a first down until midway through the second quarter, scored Penn State's first touchdown and set up its second.

"We put [the offense] in a lot of good situations and that helped them out a lot," said linebacker Tim Shaw, who had 10 tackles in his first game on the outside. "If we can score points, that's just a bonus."

The offense needed it. Penn State rushed for 264 yards, its highest total since the Akron game a year ago, but that number was bolstered by Tony Hunt's 70-yard run and Justin King's 61-yard run. Most of the time the Nittany Lions plodded ahead with quarterback keepers and quick gives to Hunt. Penn

State's 15 passing attempts was its lowest total in 19 games.

"Obviously we weren't consistent, particularly in the passing area," said Penn State head coach Joe Paterno, "but that will come, I think."

The Bulls (0-1) out-gained the Nittany Lions 279 yards to 224 after the first quarter. Trouble was, they trailed 17-0 just 21 seconds into the second quarter.

After a nine-play, 89-yard drive and 23-yard field goal from true freshman Kevin Kelly gave Penn State a 3-0 lead, South Florida quarterback Courtney Denson shook defensive end Tamba Hali and turned upfield—into the waiting arms of Shaw and middle linebacker Tyrell Sales, who popped the ball loose. Senior cornerback Alan Zemaitis scooped it up at the South Florida 16 and raced untouched into the end zone.

The teams traded punts before Pat Julmiste, in for Denson, threw an interception to safety Chris Harrell, who returned it 16 yards to the 13-yard line. Three plays later, Hunt dove over the pile for a one-yard touchdown run. The junior tailback had just four yards on his first six carries but finished with a career-high 140 on 15 carries.

"To be fair, they gave us a couple of easy ones," Paterno said. "It was a closer game than the score would indicate."

The Bulls got on the board when Julmiste (21 of 35, 200 yards) found Johnny Peyton on a fade route in the left corner of the end zone with four seconds left in the half. The six-foot-five Peyton out-jumped the six-foot King for the ball, and later beat six-foot-one senior corner Anwar Phillips on the same pattern, a four-yard score that pulled the Bulls to within 10 with 2:52 left in the game.

South Florida failed the two-point conversion try, though, and Penn State's Ethan Kilmer recovered an onside kick to seal Penn State's third straight win.

The Nittany Lions tried to show off highly touted freshmen Derrick Williams and Justin King early. Robinson's first pass went to a streaking Williams, who was knocked off stride by South

	1st	2nd	3rd	4th	Final
South Florida	0	7	0	6	13
Penn State	10	7	0	6	23

Scoring Summary

PSU—Kelly 23-yard field goal, nine plays, 89 yards in 4:05
PSU—Zemaitis 16-yard defensive fumble return (Kelly kick)
PSU—Hunt 1-yard run (Kelly kick), three plays, 13 yards in 1:07
USF—Peyton 8-yard pass from Julmiste (Benzer kick), eight plays, 55 yards in 2:00
PSU—Robinson 4-yard run (Kelly kick blocked), three plays, 79 yards in 0:54
USF—Peyton 4-yard pass from Julmiste (Julmiste pass failed), 18 plays, 85 yards in 7:14

Team Statistics

Category	USF	PSU
First Downs	17	18
Rushes-Yards (Net)	36-97	39-264
Passing Yards (Net)	200	90
Passes Att-Comp-Int	39-21-1	15-9-1
Total Offense Plays-Yards	75-297	54-354
Punt Returns-Yards	1-1	4-58
Kickoff Returns-Yards	3-60	2-34
Punts (Number-Avg)	8-45.2	5-42.2
Fumbles-Lost	1-1	4-2
Penalties-Yards	7-65	5-35
Possession Time	32:03	27:57
Sacks By (Number-Yards)	3-30	0-0

Individual Statistics

Rushing: **South Florida**-Hall 21-74; Julmiste 6-22; Ponton 4-12; Denson 2-2; Peyton 1-(-2); Carlton Hill 2-(-11).
Penn State-Hunt 15-140; King 2-66; Robinson 18-39; Golden 1-15; Williams 2-6; Team 1-(-2).

Passing: **South Florida**-Julmiste 21-35-1-200; Denson 0-3-0-0; Team 0-1-0-0.
Penn State-Robinson 9-15-1-90.

Receiving: **South Florida**-Peyton 4-39; Chambers 4-35; Hall 4-27; Green 3-32; Cedric Hill 2-38; Bleakley 1-13; Carlton Hill 1-8; Ponton 1-4; Ruegger 1-4.
Penn State-Williams 3-38; Hunt 2-16; Smolko 1-18; Kilmer 1-10; Sargeant 1-4; Scott 1-4.

Interceptions: **South Florida**-Williams 1-8.
Penn State-Harrell 1-16.

Sacks (Unassisted-Assisted): **South Florida**-Nicholas 2-0; Royal 0-1; Thomas 0-1.
Penn State-None.

Tackles (Unassisted-Assisted): **South Florida**-Team 8-2; T. Williams 4-2; Jenkins 5-0; T. Jones 4-1; St. Louis 4-1; Nicholas 4-1; Moffitt 3-2; J. Jones 2-2; Royal 1-3; Carlton Williams 2-1; Gachette 2-0; Simmons 1-1.
Penn State-Posluszny 7-3; T. Shaw 7-3; Paxson 6-1; Zemaitis 4-1; Rice 4-0; Harrell 3-1; Lowry 1-3; Sales 2-1; Hali 2-1; Gaines 1-2; Kilmer 2-0; Jim Shaw 2-0; Phillips 2-0.

ABOVE: **Tony Hunt breaks from the pack against South Florida.** *Nabil K. Mark/Centre Daily Times*
OPPOSITE PAGE: **Michael Robinson goes in for Penn State's last score.** *Nabil K. Mark/Centre Daily Times*

Florida's Mike Jenkins. Jenkins was whistled for holding, and Williams had earned 10 yards for Penn State without touching the football. The drive stalled, however, when Robinson was sacked by Stephen Nicholas and fumbled the ball away.

King's first contribution came on Penn State's next possession. The sometimes-receiver, sometimes cornerback went around left end on a reverse and raced 61 yards down the sideline before Jenkins caught him from behind.

Williams finished with 38 yards on three catches, and King had two carries for 66 yards on offense and made one tackle on defense.

"I wanted to get those kids in the game as quickly as I could," said Paterno, who had said during the week he didn't want to put too much pressure on his young receivers. Kilmer, a former

defensive back, started the game at the other wideout spot.

It was clear the Nittany Lions, who host Cincinnati next week, have plenty of work to do to integrate the new receivers into their offense. The offensive line, which welcomed new starters Lance Antolick and Robert Price, was also suspect at times.

Still, a team that has gone 4-7 and 3-9 in its last two seasons realized it isn't yet in a position to be picky.

"For us to have a game like this early, it could benefit us," said Robinson, who suffered his cut when his helmet was knocked off early in the game. "We didn't perform the way we wanted to, but it could help us in the long run."

"A win is a win," Shaw said. "A bad win is a lot better than a good loss."

GOOD AIR DAY

BY JEFF RICE

They were elated, relieved and a little smug as they talked about it, these Nittany Lions who for so long had watched their offense struggle to get out of first gear.

They had known that someday Penn State would stretch the field again, bite off huge chunks of yardage at once and flood the scoreboard with points. Saturday was their day of vindication.

Derrick Williams, Justin King and Deon Butler each caught passes of 40 yards or more and Michael Robinson threw for a career-high three touchdowns as the Nittany Lions attack looked vertical for the first time in a long time during a 42-24 win over Cincinnati before 98,727 in Beaver Stadium.

"The line did a great job. The receivers got open," said Robinson, who was 11 of 17 for 220 yards and one interception. "I had an easy job. All I had to do was put it out there and those guys ran underneath it."

After Paul Cronin recovered a Mike Daniels fumble at the Penn State 41-yard line midway through the third quarter, Robinson play-faked, dropped back and went deep down the right sideline to King. The six-foot freshman from Monroeville got behind Bearcat freshman Mike Mickens for a 59-yard touchdown, Penn State's

Deon Butler hauls in a touchdown pass against Cincinnati's Mike Mickens in the fourth quarter. Butler caught two passes for 73 yards in the game. *Craig Houtz/Centre Daily Times*

longest pass play since Matt Kranchick's 73-yarder against Wisconsin in 2003.

It didn't stop there. Cincinnati went three plays and out before Robinson, who was 4 of 9 for 44 yards in the first half, hit Williams with a 41-yard bomb down the left sideline, setting up a one-yard touchdown run from Austin Scott that put Penn State ahead 28-3.

Butler, who had picked up 28 yards on his first career catch in the second quarter, hooked up with Robinson for a 45-yard touchdown five and a half minutes into the fourth quarter.

"I think once we settled down, once Mike completed a couple passes, then we started going deep on them," said Butler, a five-foot-10 redshirt freshman from Woodbridge, Va. "We tried to force them to change their game plan but they didn't want to back up with their corners, so we just kept going down the field."

Re-establishing the deep threat, and making good on it, made the Nittany Lions' mistakes easier to forget. Penn State turned the ball over three times for the second straight week and allowed a pair of late touchdowns to end its 12-game streak of allowing 21 points or fewer.

Just as in its 23-13 win over South Florida, the Penn State defense was on the field for more than 32 minutes, but the long day at the office didn't seem as long this week.

"It's so much easier to get back on the field after a touchdown than it is after a turnover or something," said linebacker Tim Shaw, who racked up 10 tackles and a sack. "When you have that momentum with you, it's so much easier to go on the field when your offense is rolling."

The defense again did its part in fueling that momentum, turning four Cincinnati turnovers into 21 points. The Nittany Lions had Bearcats quarterback Dustin Grutza on the run all afternoon, but the gutsy redshirt freshman wriggled free again and again, throwing for 286 yards and a touchdown on 27-of-47 passing.

	1st	2nd	3rd	4th	Final
Cincinnati	0	3	7	14	24
Penn State	7	7	14	14	42

Scoring Summary

PSU—Robinson 1-yard run (Kelly kick), six plays, 25 yards in 2:10
CIN—Lovell 24-yard field goal, 14 plays, 69 yards in 5:24
PSU—Hall 3-yard pass from Robinson (Kelly kick), eight plays, 80 yards in 3:10
PSU—King 59-yard pass from Robinson (Kelly kick), one play, 59 yards in 0:08
PSU—Scott 1-yard run (Kelly kick), three plays, 47 yards in 1:07
CIN—Ross 27-yard pass from Grutza (Lovell kick), six plays, 65 yards in 3:10
PSU—Butler 45-yard pass from Robinson (Kelly kick), four plays, 71 yards in 1:25
PSU—Morelli 1-yard run (Kelly kick), 12 plays, 52 yards in 5:18
CIN—Glatthaar 2-yard run (Grutza pass failed), seven plays, 64 yards in 1:37
CIN—Jackson 5-yard pass from Davila (Jackson pass from Davila), two plays, 48 yards in 0:21

Team Statistics

Category	CIN	PSU
First Downs	23	19
Rushes-Yards (Net)	34-31	37-148
Passing Yards (Net)	329	245
Passes Att-Comp-Int	49-29-2	22-15-1
Total Offense Plays-Yards	83-360	59-393
Punt Returns-Yards	2-21	2-27
Kickoff Returns-Yards	4-86	3-61
Punts (Number-Avg)	6-38.5	4-40.8
Fumbles-Lost	4-2	2-2
Penalties-Yards	7-54	4-44
Possession Time	35:08	24:52
Sacks By (Number-Yards)	1-6	4-17

Individual Statistics

Rushing: Cincinnati-Benton 3-15; Daniels 5-13; Giddens 1-8; Moore 2-6; Glatthaar 8-3; Grutza 14-(-6); Smith 1-(-8). **Penn State**-Robinson 10-62; Hunt 11-44; Scott 10-32; Williams 3-23; Morelli 1-1; Team 1-(-1); King 1-(-13).

Passing: Cincinnati-Grutza 27-47-2-286; Davila 2-2-0-43. **Penn State**-Robinson 11-17-1-220; Morelli 4-5-0-25.

Receiving: Cincinnati-Celek 7-73; Giddens 6-44; Jackson 4-37; Daniels 4-29; Ross 3-44; Barwin 2-72; Jones 2-23; Glatthaar 1-7. **Penn State**-Williams 4-60; Butler 2-73; Hahn 2-19; Perretta 2-7; King 1-59; Smolko 1-14; Norwood 1-8; Hall 1-3; Hunt 1-2.

Interceptions: Cincinnati-Nakamura 1-0. **Penn State**-Zemaitis 1-0; Lowry 1-0.

Sacks (Unassisted-Assisted): Cincinnati-McCullough 1-0. **Penn State**-Rice 1-1; Cronin 0-1; Posluszny 1-0; T. Shaw 1-0.

Tackles (Unassisted-Assisted): Cincinnati-Nakamura 8-4; Mickens 7-1; McCullough 5-1; Smith 3-2; Roberts 2-1; Germany 2-1; Carpenter 1-2; Bowie 2-0; Williams 2-0; Hoke 0-2; Tolbert 0-2. **Penn State**-Harrell 5-6; T. Shaw 8-2; Posluszny 5-3; Sales 5-3; Lowry 5-1; Rice 4-2; Zemaitis 3-2; Cronin 2-1; Alford 1-2; Gaines 2-0; J. Cianciolo 0-2.

OPPOSITE PAGE: Derrick Williams celebrates his 41-yard pass reception to the one-yard line, which culminated in a short touchdown run by Austin Scott. *Craig Houtz/Centre Daily Times*

ABOVE: **Freshman Justin King beats Cincinnati's Mike Mickens to the end zone for a 59-yard touchdown catch.** *Michelle Klein/Centre Daily Times*
OPPOSITE PAGE: **Defensive tackle Jay Alford closes in on beleaguered Cincinnati quarterback Dustin Grutza.**
Craig Houtz/Centre Daily Times

"All week I said, 'Let's test him, make him handle some pressure,'" said Penn State head coach Joe Paterno. "And I thought he handled it well."

Penn State's backup quarterback, sophomore Anthony Morelli, also handled himself well Saturday, completing 4-of-5 passes in his season debut and scoring the Nittany Lions' final touchdown on a one-yard keeper. Tailback Tony Hunt had a workmanlike 44 yards, all in the first half, on 11 carries, while Scott chipped in 10 carries for 36 yards. Reserve tight end Patrick Hall caught his first career touchdown pass from three yards out in the first quarter.

The receivers, though, were the difference, and it went well beyond statistics. The entire offense developed a different feel, the one the Nittany Lions had hoped it would with the addition of the speedy playmakers.

That feel wasn't there in the first half. After Zemaitis picked off an ill-advised throw from Grutza at the Cincinnati 25. It took the Nittany Lions six plays—all runs—to punch it in on a one-yard sneak from Robinson. Penn State used three Cincinnati penalties to set up its second score, when Robinson made a tough rollout throw to Hall.

Other than the big catch from Butler, the Nittany Lions' offense stalled and sputtered through the first half, tallying 116 yards on just 27 plays. In the locker room at halftime, Paterno, who has tried to keep pressure off of his young receivers so far this season, told Robinson to just throw the ball and let the freshmen run under it.

The difference after that was clear.

"You saw it," said left tackle Levi Brown. "Justin came down, had a big play. We came down the next time, Derrick had a big play. The running game started opening up, and everything just got a lot easier."

"Those young guys are good athletes," Paterno said. "They work hard, they block well, they go get the football, they're courageous, they get smarter each week, and there's a little better timing developing between them and the quarterbacks."

Robinson was Penn State's lone big-play threat at receiver last season. Although it came against a green Cincinnati secondary, this performance hinted the Nittany Lions are now capable of much more.

"You can't really just key in on one receiver, because now we have three or four guys that can beat you deep," said Robinson, who completed seven of his final eight passes. "Sometimes I drop back and I don't know who to throw it to, because they can all get open."

26 TONY HUNT

BIRTHDATE: 11/24/85 **BIRTHPLACE:** SAN ANTONIO, TX **HIGH SCHOOL:** T.C. WILLIAMS (ALEXANDRIS, TX)
MAJOR: LIBERAL ARTS **POSITION:** TAILBACK **HEIGHT:** 6'2' **WEIGHT:** 219 LBS

Typically, a tailback, a quarterback or a wide receiver—all of those guys who get their hands on the football on a regular basis—will set at least one personal goal for themselves.

It might be 1,000 yards for a running back, a certain number of catches for a receiver or a particular completion percentage for the quarterbacks.

But almost always, there is something they work toward that will make the season a successful one in their opinion. They write it in their helmets, on wristbands or in notes in their lockers.

Then there is Tony Hunt.

He is in his second year as Penn State's No. 1 tailback. He knows he will get a large percentage of touches. The opportunities will be there for him to run for big yardage, score a lot of touchdowns.

Yet he needs no arbitrarily established personal goal to motivate him.

"A thousand yards is not something I think about," he explained. "I don't want to set personal goals like that for myself. If you say 1,000 yards then why not 1,500? You shortchange yourself if you just say 1,000 yards. I just go into every game and try to play my heart out.

"I just want to do whatever my role may be to get this team to win. The guys [on the team] are done with personal goals. We just want to do what it takes to get us to a big bowl game."

To some that might seem like an unreachable goal for a team that's coming off two straight losing seasons and didn't look particularly sharp in its opening game against South Florida.

Hunt emerged from that game with 140 yards and a touchdown on 15 carries. Half of those yards came on one carry, when he was caught from behind at the South Florida four by defensive

back Michael Jenkins, setting up Michael Robinson's touchdown that put the game away.

"I couldn't tell if anyone was gaining on me," he said. "That was the first time we ran that play. I don't know where the rest of the defense was. I just had one linebacker to beat, I made him miss and then I just saw a lot of open field in front of me."

Hunt's performance was one of the few bright spots in an otherwise sloppy offensive performance on opening day but he figures a lot of that can be attributed to first-game jitters.

"That was the first game so we can't be too down about it," he said. "There is plenty of time to correct the mistakes we made. We just have to make sure we don't continue to make the mistakes we made. We have to get more consistent."

One of the things Hunt has to work on is consistently holding onto the football. It's been an area of concern for Joe Paterno.

"He has to hang on to the football," Paterno said following the opener. "The one thing that I have always worried about is that he has a tendency to be careless with the football. He is a good back. If he pays attention to the little things and spends a little bit more time with tapes and watching blocking schemes and things like that he can be even better. He has speed and he is strong. He's a 225-pound tailback."

One of the things Hunt worked on, at Paterno's urging, was increasing his conditioning, which in turn would make him better on Saturday afternoons. Based on what has happened to this point in the season, Hunt has picked up the gauntlet Paterno threw down.

"I challenged him because I think he can be really good," Paterno added. "I think Tony has responded very well."

That 70-yard dash was the second-longest run of his Penn State career. He got loose for a 77-yard scoring run against Akron a year ago when he finished the year as the team's leading rusher with 777 yards on 169 carries.

It's a sign of the maturation process.

"He's a more patient runner now," said quarterback Michael Robinson. "Now, he lets things open up and then he hits them. Before he waited too long. Now, he hits them exactly when he's supposed to hit them. He has made great improvement, even from last year to this. He will be a big part of this offense this year."

For Hunt, that's a considerable compliment given that Hunt was a fresh-faced freshman when Robinson took Hunt under his wing.

"I would be in the game and there were times when I wouldn't know who I had, what I was supposed to do," Hunt said, "and he helped me out."

Hunt came to Penn State from T.C. Williams High in Alexandria, Virginia, the school made famous in *Remember the Titans*. There he ran for 2,794 yards and scored 30 touchdowns.

What he didn't know, and didn't care about, was that there were two other outstanding high school tailbacks in his recruiting class—Austin Scott and Rodney Kinlaw.

"I didn't think about who else was coming here," he said. "If you go to a top university there are going to be top recruits. I didn't compare myself to the other guys.

"What matters is what you do out on this practice field. It doesn't matter what you did before."

What did matter was the difference in how a Division I-A program is run compared to a high-powered high school one; it caught him off guard.

"Everything is so structured here," he said. "I had to get used to the fact that everything is so disciplined. Everything is so strict. It's totally different from high school."

The stakes are also a little higher. There's no bowl game awaiting a high school team at the end of its season. The best it can hope for is making it to the state playoffs. Penn State can get a bowl bid just by winning six games. But Hunt has his sights set higher than that even though the Nittany Lions have not been to a bowl since he arrived.

"I pretty much figured it (going to a bowl) would be automatic," he admitted. "I figured there was no way we weren't going to a bowl, it was just a matter of which one we were going to.

"No one wants to lose. We haven't been to a bowl in my first two years here and no one is happy about that. We know what we have to do this year."

By Ron Bracken

Adam Bueb/Centre Daily Times

SACKS APPEAL

BY JEFF RICE

B low enough things up in the middle, and it won't be long until all sides come crashing down.

Tackles Scott Paxson and Jay Alford lit the charges and the rest of Penn State's defensive line took it from there during a brisk 40-3 demolition of Central Michigan in Beaver Stadium.

The Nittany Lions' front four recorded five of Penn State's eight sacks—the team's highest total in five years—and held the Chippewas to 14 yards rushing on 39 attempts.

"Once you see that you can get a good push up the field, then that's pretty much the ball game," said Alford, who finished with three tackles and one sack. "If your two inside guys are working, that pretty much makes everybody else's job easy."

It was open season on Chippewas quarterback Kent Smith, the tall left-hander who had set a school total offense record with 478 yards the week before in a 38-37 win at Miami of Ohio. Tamba Hali, who had spent most of Penn State's first two games in the backfield but had come up empty-handed, had two and a half sacks and three of 16 Penn State tackles for loss.

RIGHT: Senior safety Paul Cronin tackles Central Michigan's Justin Harper.
Nabil K. Mark/Centre Daily Times

ABOVE: **Quarterback Michael Robinson gains positive yardage against Central Michigan's defense. Robinson gave the Nittany Lions their first touchdown of the game on a keeper.** *Nabil K. Mark/Centre Daily Times*

"Tamba Hali does not get enough credit," said Penn State coach Joe Paterno. "We've had some great defensive ends around here, and he'd be right there with Courtney Brown and all of them."

Smith completed 23-of-36 passes but for only 143 yards. With Paxson, Alford and reserve Steve Roach shutting down the Central Michigan running game and ends Hali, Matthew Rice and Josh Gaines flying in from the outside, the

Chippewas struggled to get much of anything accomplished.

The most criticized unit of a standout Penn State defense, one that was dealt serious blows this summer with the expulsion of tackle Ed Johnson, the transfer of end Amani Purcell and the academic ineligibility of end Lavon Chisley, responded in a big way.

"All we've been talking about was 'Push it,'" Hali said. "If they're gonna step up, you guys get the play, if they step back, we get the play. We were just working as a collective group today."

Contrast Smith's afternoon with that had by Penn State quarterback Michael Robinson, who was rarely bothered as he threw for three touchdowns and ran for another. The senior tri-captain finished 14 of 23 for 274 yards and gave way to Anthony Morelli, who threw for 107 yards and a touchdown, midway through the third quarter.

Before an announced crowd of 100,276—Beaver Stadium's first 100,000-plus crowd in three games this season—the Nittany Lions improved to 3-0 for the first time in three seasons by rolling up 519 yards of total offense. Penn State's 381 yards passing were the most it has had in a game since Zack Mills threw for 399 in 2002.

Redshirt freshman receiver Deon Butler was the star of the day with five catches for 108 yards, two for touchdowns, and junior tailback Tony Hunt churned out 78 yards on 10 carries.

More impressive, though, was a defense that allowed just 172 yards in 77 plays. The Nittany Lions fell three sacks short of the school record, set against Illinois in 1999, and matched their eight-sack performance against Michigan State in 2000.

"I love it, man," said cornerback Alan Zemaitis. "The defensive line and the secondary work hand in hand. If we cover, they sack. If they get some pressure, we pick it."

The Chippewas (1-2) were the first team to play a turnover-free game against the Nittany Lions this season but had just five plays of 10 yards or more and just five possessions of 20 yards or more. Showing off their new offensive weapons once again, the Nittany Lions had eight plays or 20 yards or more.

"Here's what Penn State now has. They have balance in their offense," said Central Michigan coach Brian Kelly. "If they couldn't throw the ball down the field they would have struggled today, like they did last year at times. Their ability now to match up their secondary without much help puts us in a very bad situation. Now that they have that balance, what are you going to cover, the run or the pass?"

	1st	2nd	3rd	4th	Final
Central Michigan	0	3	0	0	3
Penn State	7	19	7	7	40

Scoring Summary
PSU—Robinson 2-yard run (Kelly kick), five plays, 77 yards in 2:10
PSU—Kelly 33-yard field goal, six plays, 50 yards in 2:18
PSU—Butler 54-yard pass from Robinson (Kelly kick failed), two plays, 80 yards in 0:42
PSU—Butler 24-yard pass from Robinson (Kelly kick), three plays, 43 yards in 0:56
CMU—Albreski 31-yard field goal, four plays, zero yards in 1:47
PSU—Kelly 37-yard field goal, three plays, 18 yards in 0:24
PSU—Golden 47-yard pass from Robinson (Kelly kick), six plays, 81 yards in 1:41
PSU—Kilmer 55-yard pass from Morelli (Kelly kick), three plays, 61 yards in 0:41

Team Statistics
Category	CMU	PSU
First Downs	13	26
Rushes-Yards (Net)	39-14	31-138
Passing Yards (Net)	158	381
Passes Att-Comp-Int	38-25-0	36-22-1
Total Offense Plays-Yards	77-172	67-519
Punt Returns-Yards	0-0	5-37
Kickoff Returns-Yards	5-103	2-62
Punts (Number-Avg)	11-42.1	4-36.5
Fumbles-Lost	1-0	3-2
Penalties-Yards	9-74	4-29
Possession Time	31:41	28:19
Sacks By (Number-Yards)	3-19	8-71

Individual Statistics
Rushing: **Central Michigan**-Sneed 12-32; Boykins 8-21; Smith 19-(-39). **Penn State**-Hunt 10-78; Pinchek 4-15; Scott 4-15; Robinson 5-13; King 2-9; Williams 1-9; Kinlaw 1-4; Lawlor 1-4; Morelli 3-(-9).

Passing: **Central Michigan**-Smith 23-36-0-143; Brunner 2-2-0-15. **Penn State**-Robinson 14-23-1-274; Morelli 8-13-0-107.

Receiving: **Central Michigan**-Linson 6-46; Harper 6-24; Cetoute 3-32; Sneed 3-28; Brown 2-11; Jasmin 2-4; Gardner 1-11; Jean 1-4; Boykins 1-(-2). **Penn State**-Butler 5-108; Perretta 3-32; Norwood 3-17; Kilmer 2-64; Williams 2-47; Hunt 2-36; Golden 1-47; Smolko 1-21; Snow 1-5; Kinlaw 1-3; King 1-1.

Interceptions: **Central Michigan**-Keith 1-0. **Penn State**-None.

Sacks (Unassisted-Assisted): **Central Michigan**-Bazuin 2-0; Williams 1-0. **Penn State**-Hali 2-1; Shaw 2-0; Alford 0-2; Paxson 0-1; Rice 1-0; Lowry 1-0.

Tackles (Unassisted-Assisted): **Central Michigan**-Jackson 7-2; Williams 4-3; Kress 4-2; Maxwell 4-2; Keith 2-4; Bazuin 4-1; Brown 3-2; Smith 4-0; Horne 1-2; Dailey 2-0; Wohlgamuth 1-1; Ruger 1-1; Ball 1-1; Cutts 1-1. **Penn State**-T. Shaw 8-2; Lowry 5-3; Posluszny 5-3; Phillips 6-1; Ridenhour 4-2; Paxson 3-2; Cronin 4-0; Harrell 3-1; Hali 2-2; Zemaitis 3-0; Rice 2-1; Alford 1-2; Brown 2-0; Lucian 2-0; King 1-1.

ABOVE: **Senior defensive end Matt Rice tackles CMU's Anthony Boykins for a loss. The Nittany Lions' defense held Central Michigan to 172 total offensive yards in the game.** *Nabil K. Mark/Centre Daily Times*

Relentless junior defensive end Daniel Bazuin had two of Central Michigan's three sacks and forced a fumble, one of three Penn State turnovers, but didn't get much help from his teammates as the young Nittany Lions wide receivers displayed their big-play ability for the second straight week.

Butler helped Penn State pull away in the second quarter, beating Vincent Hicks on a post pattern for a 54-yard touchdown grab, then getting behind Curtis Cutts for a 24-yard touchdown two and a half minutes later to make it 23-0 with 2:57 left in the half.

"That's all a tribute to the coaching staff making great calls," said Butler, one of three freshmen who have revitalized Penn State's passing attack. "They weren't great catches, everything was just wide open."

Terrell Golden chipped in with a very wide-open 47-yard touchdown grab early in the third quarter, his first catch of the season and just the fourth of his career, and Ethan Kilmer completed Penn State's scoring with a 55-yard catch-and-run, his first career score, with six minutes to play.

The Nittany Lions struck quickly on their first possession. Hunt caught a pass from Robinson and tore up the right sideline for 28 yards, then added a 39-yard run on the next play to set up first-and-goal. Robinson went in from two yards out two plays later. A 39-yard completion to Derrick Williams on the next possession set up a 33-yard field goal by Kevin Kelly, who was 2 of 3 on field goals on the afternoon.

Penn State visits Northwestern on September 24 to begin Big Ten play. The Nittany Lions have just one road win and three conference wins in their last two seasons.

"We're doing some things pretty good," Paterno said, "but whether we're good enough to beat some of the real good teams we have coming up remains to be seen."

ABOVE: Tamba Hali takes down quarterback Kent Smith in the third quarter. Hali had two and a half sacks on the night. *Nabil K. Mark/Centre Daily Times*

"*Tamba Hali does not get enough credit. We've had some great defensive ends around here, and he'd be right there with Courtney Brown and all of them.*"

— Joe Paterno, Penn State coach

NEW KIDS ON THE CLOCK

BY JEFF RICE

A t the conclusion of every practice, Penn State assistant coaches Mike McQueary and Jay Paterno pop an old videotape in the VCR for their young wide receivers. As the players cool down, they watch the great last-minute drives and unforgettable plays of Nittany Lions offenses past.

The remarkable march at Illinois in 1994. Bobby Engram's catch to beat Michigan State the following year. Chafie Fields' catch down the sideline to shock Miami in 1999.

Down to their last play in their first venture away from University Park, the new kids added to that tape on September 24.

Senior quarterback Michael Robinson led the Nittany Lions 80 yards in one minute, 19 seconds, hitting freshman Derrick Williams for a 36-yard touchdown with 51 seconds left to give Penn State a memorable, come-from-behind 34-29 win over Northwestern.

"This is what we work out for," said Robinson, who threw for 271 yards and completed four of his final five passes. "This is why we put in all the hours. This is what we came to Penn State for."

The Nittany Lions (4-0, 1-0 Big Ten) battled back from a 23-7 second-quarter deficit to take a one-point lead in the fourth quarter and then answered right back after the Wildcats (2-2, 0-1)

regained the lead on Joel Howells' fifth field goal of the afternoon with 2:10 remaining.

Penn State's final drive didn't seem destined for the highlight reel at first. Robinson just missed Williams near the sideline, then was sacked by Northwestern's Barry Cofield and fumbled for the fourth time. Tony Hunt recovered, but Penn State faced a fourth-and-15 from its own 15 after a Robinson-to-Hunt completion lost two yards.

On fourth down, Robinson, who threw three interceptions and lost a fumble, stepped up in the pocket and hit Isaac Smolko down the middle for a 20-yard gain.

Five plays later, he fluttered a high pass down the left sideline. Williams grabbed it, ducked under the grasp of Wildcats safety Reggie McPherson and trotted into the end zone for his first career score, sending the Penn State sideline into a frenzy and stunning the sparse Ryan Field crowd of 24,395.

"That's something that everybody dreams for," said Williams, speaking to the media for the first time since the season started. "Especially, my first touchdown."

OPPOSITE PAGE: **Penn State cornerback Alan Zemaitis takes down quarterback Brett Basanez on a draw play in the fourth quarter.**
Brian Bahr/Getty Images

There was still time for Northwestern and fearless quarterback Brett Basanez, but his first pass went directly into the arms of Penn State's Anwar Phillips, Basanez's first interception in 143 attempts.

That stop—just the fifth time Penn State's defense had halted Northwestern all afternoon—marked the end to a wild back-and-forth battle that saw the Wildcats dominate early and both teams squander late chances to put the game away.

Coming off a brutal 52-21 loss at Arizona State, Northwestern dominated the first quarter, taking a 10-0 lead and out-gaining the Nittany Lions 155-11 in total yardage. The Wildcats, which saw their eight-game winning streak at Ryan Field snapped, added another field goal four seconds into the second quarter thanks to a bizarre special-teams play.

Howells' kickoff fluttered to the 15, then bounced backward to the 26, where the Wildcats' Ben Rothrauff pounced on it before the Nittany Lions knew what happened.

But Penn State's defense stiffened and the Wildcats had to settle for another field goal by Howells.

The Nittany Lions offense, which had 11 yards in seven plays to that point, came alive. Williams' roommate, freshman Justin King, caught a 37-yard touchdown from Robinson to cap a seven-play, 80-yard drive.

The Nittany Lions appeared to have fully seized the momentum when Jason Ganter forced and recovered a fumble (again at the 26-yard line) on the ensuing kickoff, but they gave it right back when a Robinson's pass was tipped and intercepted by Adam Kadela.

Basanez, who was 20 of 38 for 229 yards, hit Jonathan Fields with a 38-yard strike to set up Tyrell Sutton's second one-yard touchdown run of the day. Another Robinson interception led to a Howells' third field goal to make it 23-7, but

	1st	2nd	3rd	4th	Final
Penn State	0	14	3	17	34
Northwestern	10	13	0	6	29

Scoring Summary

NU—Sutton 1-yard run (Howells kick), 16 plays, 80 yards in 5:52
NU—Howells 20-yard field goal, 10 plays, 52 yards in 3:51
NU—Howells 25-yard field goal, six plays, 18 yards in 2:10
PSU—King 37-yard pass from Robinson (Kelly kick), seven plays, 80 yards in 2:36
NU—Sutton 1-yard run (Howells kick), 10 plays, 71 yards in 3:54
NU—Howells 42-yard field goal, four plays, minus-eight yards in 1:24
PSU—Butler 26-yard pass from Robinson (Kelly kick), eight plays, 61 yards in 1:16
PSU—Kelly 25-yard field goal, five plays, 31 yards in 1:29
PSU—Kelly 28-yard field goal, eight plays, 61 yards in 2:21
NU—Howells 46-yard field goal, 12 plays, 42 yards in 3:58
PSU—Robinson 8-yard run (Kelly kick), five plays, 77 yards in 1:23
NU—Howells 25-yard field goal, 16 plays, 86 yards in 6:42
PSU—Williams 36-yard pass from Robinson (Kelly kick), nine plays, 80 yards in 1:19

Team Statistics

Category	PSU	NU
First Downs	21	24
Rushes-Yards (Net)	27-209	57-198
Passing Yards (Net)	271	229
Passes Att-Comp-Int	36-17-3	38-20-1
Total Offense Plays-Yards	63-480	95-427
Punt Returns-Yards	2-15	0-0
Kickoff Returns-Yards	4-98	5-107
Punts (Number-Avg)	2-49.0	3-34.3
Fumbles-Lost	4-1	1-1
Penalties-Yards	5-50	6-35
Possession Time	20:01	39:59
Sacks By (Number-Yards)	2-8	1-3

Individual Statistics

Rushing: Penn State-Hunt 13-99; Robinson 9-60; King 1-43; Williams 3-9; Team 1-(-2).
Northwestern-Sutton 32-112; Basanez 21-54; Pederson 1-19; Hamlett 2-10; Fields 1-3.

Passing: Penn State-Robinson 17-36-3-271.
Northwestern-Basanez 20-38-1-229.

Receiving: Penn State-Norwood 5-83; Butler 4-61; Hunt 4-28; Williams 2-42; King 1-37; Smolko 1-20.
Northwestern-Herbert 7-47; Fields 4-70; Sutton 3-32; Philmore 3-27; Abernathy 1-20; Lane 1-17; Thompson 1-16.

Interceptions: Penn State-Phillips 1-7.
Northwestern-Simpson 1-10; Kadela 1-7; Cole 1-21.

Sacks (Unassisted-Assisted): Penn State-Hali 0-2; Paxson 0-1; Alford 0-1.
Northwestern-Cofield 1-0.

Tackles (Unassisted-Assisted): Penn State-Posluszny 14-8; Lowry 7-5; Harrell 4-4; T. Shaw 4-4; Rice 3-5; Cronin 3-4; Paxson 2-4; Hali 2-4; Connor 2-3; Phillips 2-2; Alford 1-3; Zemaitis 1-3; Golden 2-0; J. Cianciolo 2-0.
Northwestern-McGarigle 7-2; Smith 3-6; Henderson 7-1; McPherson 1-5; Simpson 1-4; Cofield 1-2; Cole 1-1; Mims 1-1; Conteh 1-1; Roach 1-1; Kadela 0-2; Schultz 0-2.

OPPOSITE PAGE: Wide receiver Derrick Williams celebrates his 36-yard touchdown in the fourth quarter. With only 51 seconds left in the game, the touchdown put Penn State ahead for the win over Northwestern 34-29.
Brian Bahr/Getty Images

Northwestern never delivered the knockout punch in the first half.

A 26-yard strike from Robinson to Deon Butler drew the Nittany Lions within nine late in the second quarter. Freshmen pulled in 12 of Penn State's 17 catches for 223 yards and three touchdowns, including a team-high five catches for 83 yards from State College graduate Jordan Norwood.

Penn State's defense, which had allowed just 47.3 yards rushing in its first three games and 99 in the first half, regrouped in the locker room.

"The first half we were just trying too many different things," said linebacker Paul Posluszny, who finished with 22 tackles. "In the second half, we just lined up and played football. That seemed to work really well for us."

And, while still sloppy with the football, Robinson and the offense started to find the holes in a Wildcats defense that surrendered 773 yards the week before. A pair of field goals by Kevin Kelly narrowed the gap to 23-20, and Penn State finally took a 27-26 lead when Robinson ran it in from eight yards out with just less than nine minutes to play.

Basanez wasn't done yet, though. The Penn State defense, on the field for a full two-thirds of the game, started to wear down late, and the Wildcats started to take advantage of the over-pursuing Nittany Lions with screen passes and option gives to Sutton.

"It's an offense you barely see around the country," said Penn State cornerback Alan Zemaitis. "And when they do run that kind of offense, they always have success with it. An incredible system they've got, Northwestern."

Penn State could have effectively ended the game even sooner, but a late hit out-of-bounds by safety Chris Harrell prolonged the Wildcats' drive. Basanez and Sutton (32 carries, 112 yards)

LEFT: **Fullback BranDon Snow lifts up quarterback Michael Robinson after Robinson led the Nittany Lions to a come-from-behind victory.**
Brian Bahr/Getty Images

drove the Wildcats to the Penn State five-yard line, but Scott Paxson made a huge stop of Basanez on third-and-four. Northwestern had to settle for a 25-yard field goal from Howells, which set the stage for Robinson, Smolko and Williams.

Penn State won on the road for just the second time in 14 games and snapped a two-game losing streak to Northwestern.

"This was a very emotional game," Smolko said. "It was a better victory than if we'd just blown them out. We needed this kind of win to boost our team."

"Obviously, we are in a stage of getting good and I think you only get good when you overcome some adversity," Penn State coach Joe Paterno said. "And I think they had some adversity today and they hung in there."

"This was a very emotional game. It was a better victory than if we'd just blown them out. We needed this kind of win to boost our team."

—Isaac Smolko, wide receiver

RIGHT: Penn State cornerback Anwar Phillips celebrates his interception of a Brett Basanez pass in the final seconds of the game to seal the win over Northwestern.
Brian Bahr/Getty Images

ROBINSON WANTS TO FORGET, REMEMBER NU GAME

BY JEFF RICE

In many ways, it was a game he probably doesn't want to remember—three interceptions, four fumbles (only one lost), just a 50 percent completion percentage and at least one overthrow he would like back.

The final drive, the final throw, the final numbers on the scoreboard, though, Michael Robinson will never forget.

This is why the player who will never go down as the best quarterback in Penn State history, only as the most patient, most positive, most resilient and most delightfully imperfect came to play for Joe Paterno. Why he stayed, even when stuck firmly between a rock (Zack Mills) and a rocket arm (Anthony Morelli). Why he took upon himself the burden of reviving a lame-duck offense and leading the team—the whole team—back to where he thought it should be.

Nine plays, 80 yards, one touchdown, one immeasurably important comeback win.

No, this 34-29 win at Northwestern wasn't a display of quarterbacking proficiency. There were the three picks, the fumbles, the missed connections to the streaking receivers. He fessed up quickly to the media afterward, but during the game, Robinson didn't sulk, didn't point fingers, just kept playing.

"To us, he was all positive," said freshman wide receiver Deon Butler, who caught four passes for 61 yards. "He knows if he gets down on himself, that we have a lot of young receivers and we'll probably start to get down on each other too."

He didn't, and they didn't, and somehow Robinson and his offense and the defense squirmed and scratched and clawed their way back into a game they probably shouldn't have been in, and thrust him directly into the spot he's always dreamed of: final drive, two minutes to play, one timeout, a score to win.

It came on the same field that kick-started his predecessor's career. Mills entered the game in Evanston late in 2001, calmly assembled the huddle, asked his teammates if they were ready to score and then led them to one, the game-winner. Robinson, now the unquestioned starter after so many games as a receiver or a runner or a clipboard holder, pushed his previous struggles out of his memory. He saw a little over two minutes and one timeout remaining, a Northwestern defense waiting to be picked apart, and an opportunity to get the sort of win his team desperately needed.

"He looked us dead in the eye and said, 'What kind of football team do we want to be?'" Butler said.

For the first three plays, the Nittany Lions looked as if they weren't sure how to answer that question. An incompletion. A sack. A doomed screen pass to Tony Hunt that lost two yards.

OPPOSITE PAGE: **Quarterback Michael Robinson maintained a positive outlook during the ups and downs of the Northwestern game. His legacy will be his patient and resilient leadership.**
Nabil K. Mark/Centre Daily Times

> **"Days like this were a moment for him to shine. And that's what he did out there."**
>
> **—Alan Zemaitis, cornerback**

And then, on fourth down and forever, 20 yards to Isaac Smolko. Eleven to Butler. Thirteen to Butler. Precision, timing, poise. Strong, accurate passes.

"It almost felt kind of like practice," Butler recalled. "Just a little more tired."

On second down from the 40, Robinson was flushed out of the pocket. He had a couple of choices—tuck it in and turn upfield, try to force the ball to a covered receiver or, the choice he made—scrambling for a few yards and stepping wisely out of bounds. The old Robinson, the score-on-every-play Robinson, might not have made that decision.

"Mike just showed us that he can lead us to a win today," Butler said. "He was hitting everybody on the money the last drive when it really counted."

On third-and-six from the Northwestern 36, all Robinson needed was 10, maybe 15 more yards to put Kevin Kelly in position for the game-winning field goal. That would not have fit this drive, though. The heave to Derrick Williams, who couldn't have picked a better time to chalk up his first career touchdown, fit it perfectly. It wasn't a pretty pass, but then, a pretty pass wouldn't have fit, either.

"That last drive was all heart," Robinson said.

It was, and most of it was Robinson's. His freshman receivers have injected speed, confidence and a little swagger into this team, but the quarterback thus far has kept it on line.

Later, Robinson quoted Frederick Douglass: "There can be no progress without struggle."

Perhaps better than any other Penn State quarterback, Robinson understands struggle. It was what made this imperfect progress all the sweeter.

"Days like this were a moment for him to shine," said Alan Zemaitis, the senior cornerback and confidant who has seen Robinson through it all. "And that's what he did out there."

Thanks to their quarterback, the Nittany Lions now know what kind of football team they want to be. This game showed it doesn't have to be a perfect one.

OPPOSITE PAGE: **Quarterback Michael Robinson fires a pass downfield. Robinson threw three interceptions against Northwestern, but none was returned for touchdowns.** *Brian Bahr/Getty Images*

CLUBBED 'SOTA

BY JEFF RICE

One team was supposed to roll up 300 yards rushing, control the line of scrimmage and the clock and stay unbeaten atop a wide-open Big Ten, and one team did.

It just wasn't the one everyone expected it to be.

With draws and dives and reverses and the option, Penn State's offense defeated No. 18 Minnesota at its own game, while the Nittany Lions defense sent Laurence Maroney and the nation's top rushing attack home with barely a whimper during a 44-14 win before 106,604 in Beaver Stadium.

Tony Hunt had 114 yards on 21 carries and two touchdowns, quarterback Michael Robinson ran for a career-high 112 yards on 18 carries and freshman sensation Derrick Williams, fitting right in at tailback, added 40 yards and a pair of touchdowns for Penn State (5-0, 2-0 Big Ten). The Nittany Lions piled up 364 yards on the ground and held the ball for 91 plays and more than 35 minutes. Maroney, the nation's leading rusher entering the game, was held to 48 yards—127 below his average—on 16 carries as the Golden Gophers (4-1, 1-1) had just 113 yards on 32 carries.

"We kind of live by the run," said Minnesota coach Glen Mason. "I guess if you don't run the ball, you die by the run."

Penn State's Ethan Kilmer celebrates after stuffing Minnesota's Laurence Maroney on the opening kickoff. *Craig Houtz/Centre Daily Times*

ABOVE: Receiver Deon Butler hauls in a long pass from Michael Robinson for a first down, in spite of Minnesota's Trumaine Banks' best efforts to stop him. *Craig Houtz/Centre Daily Times*

How dominant was Penn State in this one? Minnesota didn't pick up a first down until midway through the second quarter—the Nittany Lions already had 12 at that point and finished with 35, the second-highest total under coach Joe Paterno.

"I thought we played a good football game—everywhere," said Paterno, who snapped a four-game losing streak to Mason and Minnesota and watched his team play its first turnover-free game of the season.

Both teams were coming off exhausting wins the week before—Penn State at Northwestern, Minnesota over Purdue. The Nittany Lions had far more bounce from the beginning, jumping to a 20-0 lead and putting a chokehold on the game with back-to-back touchdown drives to start the third quarter.

Robinson had a solid if inconsistent day in the pocket (13 of 32, 175 yards, no touchdowns or interceptions) but shredded the Gophers defense as a runner, taking what the defense gave him—mostly the quarterback draw—and even knocking Minnesota safety Brandon Owens out of the game with a huge hit on a second-quarter carry.

With the Gophers taking away the deep routes, Robinson and Penn State's wide receivers worked the underneath routes and the Nittany Lions running attack hit Minnesota's six-man front from all angles.

"It depends on what people want to do to us," Paterno said. "If they want to take the passing game away from us, you gotta run the ball. I don't know what the figures were today, but we were fairly balanced, I think."

If Penn State didn't show much balance between run and pass—364 yards to 175—it was plenty balanced within the running game. Austin Scott had 54 yards on nine carries, Rodney Kinlaw scored his first touchdown of the season on a 10-yard jaunt and Justin King made the most of his only touch of the day, picking up 19 yards on an end-around in the third quarter.

Williams was the unexpected weapon out of the backfield, though, and got Penn State off to a

quick start, taking an option pitch from Robinson—and nearly dropping it—and darting 13 yards into the end zone to give Penn State a 7-0 lead on its first possession.

	1st	2nd	3rd	4th	Final
Minnesota	0	7	0	7	14
Penn State	10	10	17	7	44

Scoring Summary
PSU—Williams 13-yard run (Kelly kick), nine plays, 64 yards in 4:08
PSU—Kelly 29-yard field goal, 13 plays, 67 yards in 3:47
PSU—Williams 5-yard run (Kelly kick), 13 plays, 66 yards in 5:33
PSU—Kelly 47-yard field goal, five plays, 23 yards in 0:46
MINN—Wheelwright 48-yard pass from Cupito (Giannini kick), three plays, 57 yards in 1:17
PSU—Hunt 5-yard run (Kelly kick), nine plays, 76 yards in 3:09
PSU—Hunt 3-yard run (Kelly kick), six plays, 54 yards in 1:15
PSU—Kelly 21-yard field goal, 13 plays, 74 yards in 4:45
MINN—Wallace 2-yard run (Giannini kick), 16 plays, 73 yards in 6:03
PSU—Kinlaw 10-yard run (Kelly kick), 11 plays, 80 yards in 5:47

Team Statistics
Category	MINN	PSU
First Downs	13	35
Rushes-Yards (Net)	32-113	59-364
Passing Yards (Net)	174	175
Passes Att-Comp-Int	28-16-1	32-13-0
Total Offense Plays-Yards	60-287	91-539
Punt Returns-Yards	1-(-4)	2-8
Kickoff Returns-Yards	8-179	2-37
Punts (Number-Avg)	4-45.5	2-42.0
Fumbles-Lost	2-1	1-0
Penalties-Yards	4-54	3-15
Possession Time	24:42	35:18
Sacks By (Number-Yards)	0-0	1-5

Individual Statistics
Rushing: **Minnesota**-Russell 8-53; Maroney 16-48; Cupito 6-16; Wallace 2-(-4). **Penn State**-Hunt 21-114; Robinson 18-112; Scott 9-52; Williams 6-40; King 1-19; Kinlaw 3-15; Hahn 1-12.

Passing: **Minnesota**-Cupito 16-28-1-174. **Penn State**-Robinson 13-32-0-175.

Receiving: **Minnesota**-Wallace 5-63; Spaeth 3-21; Wheelwright 2-62; Ellerson 2-15; Payne 2-10; Maroney 2-3. **Penn State**-Butler 6-83; Williams 4-32; Smolko 1-25; Golden 1-19; Norwood 1-16.

Interceptions: **Minnesota**-None. **Penn State**-Davis 1-0.

Sacks (Unassisted-Assisted): **Minnesota**-None. **Penn State**-Alford 1-0.

Tackles (Unassisted-Assisted): **Minnesota**-Pawielski 8-4; Shevlin 6-4; Sherels 6-1; VanDeSteeg 3-4; Harris 4-2; Montgomery 2-4; Banks 4-1; Lipka 2-3; Owens 2-3; Davis 2-3; Barber 2-2; Meisel 1-2; Losli 0-3; Allen 1-1; Clark 0-2. **Penn State**-Lowry 6-3; Posluszny 2-7; Harrell 3-5; Hali 1-6; T. Shaw 3-3; Connor 2-3; Rice 2-2; J. Cianciolo 1-3; Zemaitis 2-1; Alford 1-2; Brown 1-1; Hardy 1-1; Paxson 0-2.

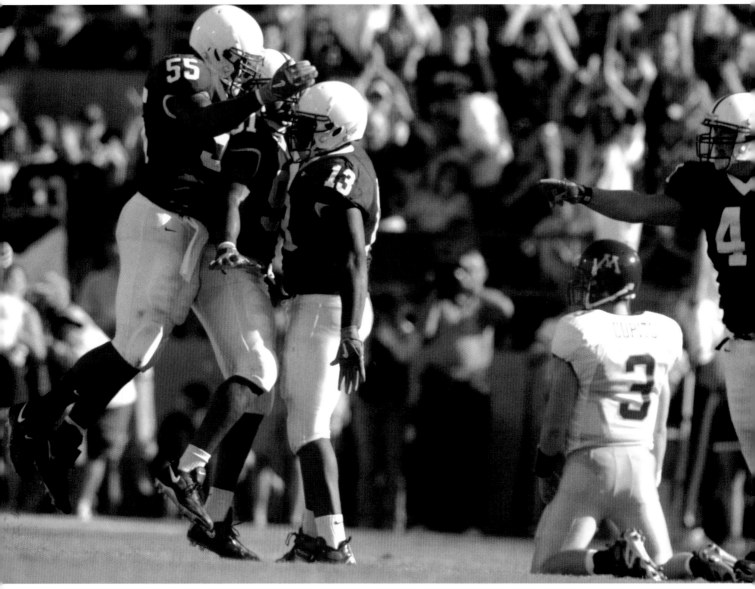

ABOVE: **Matthew Rice (55), Tamba Hali (91), Jay Alford (13) and Scott Paxson (41) celebrate Alford's sack of Minnesota quarterback Bryan Cupito (3). The sack forced a field goal attempt, which failed.**
Michelle Klein/Centre Daily Times

"I just caught it and left it there for a little while," said Williams, who added four receptions for 32 yards. "And then I saw an opening and just tried to hit it full-speed."

He found another opening early in the second quarter. Robinson, who ran for 87 yards in the first half, looked as if he were headed through the middle on another draw, but instead flipped it to a curling Williams on another end-around. The freshman

picked up a nice block from left guard Charles Rush and coasted into the end zone from five yards out to put Penn State ahead 17-0.

"We have a lot of stuff that we can do," Williams said, "and a lot of key players that can come in at any time and break the game open."

Freshman Kevin Kelly accounted for the Nittany Lions' other first-half points, hitting field goals of 29 and a career-high 47 yards, and

Minnesota got on the board when Bryan Cupito (16 of 28, 174 yards, one interception) found wideout Ernie Wheelwright on a 48-yard touchdown strike with 1:43 left before the half.

A nine-play, 76-yard scoring drive capped by a five-yard touchdown run from Hunt and a six-play, 54-yard drive capped by a three-yard touchdown from Hunt sandwiched a brisk five-play-and-out drive by Minnesota, and the Golden Gophers were ready to board the buses.

"They were a better team than I gave them credit for," Cupito said. "They controlled the game and their defense played the best I've seen in two years against us. They just shut down the run completely."

After allowing season highs in points and yardage the week before against Northwestern, the Penn State defense was brutish and businesslike, allowing only 60 plays and 287 total yards to the nation's No. 5 overall offense.

"Today didn't even compare to last game," said linebacker Paul Posluszny. "In the beginning of the game it felt like we should be out there more. It didn't seem like we were on the field long enough."

That's because the Penn State offense, its senior quarterback cool, calm and careful with the football, didn't seem to want to leave the field Saturday.

"Robinson makes it all easier," Paterno said.

On this day, against a team that had been anything but easy the last few seasons, the Nittany Lions showed Minnesota how easy the game can be when you run the football.

BELOW: Minnesota quarterback Bryan Cupito is tackled by sophomore linebacker Dan Connor in the second quarter. *Jason Malmont/Centre Daily Times*

FINALLY, A BUDDING RIVALRY

BY JEFF RICE

It's not a big game because Lee Corso is here. It's not a big game because it's No. 6 vs. No. 16. It's not a big game because 110,000 people will have had the whole day to, um, get happy, or because about 100 of them have made Beaver Stadium their temporary home since October 2.

It's a big game, Penn State fans, because it's Ohio State.

Do you really need any more reason than that?

The Nittany Lions have waited for an honest-to-goodness Big Ten rivalry to emerge since they joined the conference in 1993, and if any team currently fits the mold, it is the hated Buckeyes of the west.

Particularly this season. Penn State fans have seen the scarlet-and-gray enemy, and it is themselves. They have a big stadium. (Hey! *We* have a big stadium!) They have great linebackers. (Hey! *We* have great linebackers!) They have a national championship in the last five years (Hey! *We* have great linebackers!).

Trouble is the Buckeyes only have so much animosity to give the Nittany Lions. They have to make sure there's enough stored away at season's end for their game against a certain other interstate rival.

"I wouldn't say it's bigger than Michigan," Buckeyes safety Donte Whitner said this week, "but the rivalry is there."

That could explain why the normally low-key Buckeyes couldn't resist taking a couple of pokes at Penn State in the Columbus papers. Ohio State has been the favorite in each of the last five meetings, winning four of those games, but Penn State has won four of its last six games against the Buckeyes in Beaver Stadium, and it would have been five had David Kimball's field goal been one more yard left and two more yards longer two seasons ago.

Something about those white jerseys under gray helmets doesn't sit well with the Nittany Lions. That 2-6 team in 2003 had little business being on the field with the defending national champions, but played its brains out and probably should have won.

The teams meet October 8 with a combined 8-1 record, but it doesn't matter what the records are. They were a combined 6-8 when they met in Columbus last season, but you couldn't tell that to the Nittany Lions.

"That game was still huge to us," said Penn State tailback Tony Hunt. "Everything that's going on with this game is huge."

"It's two states going after each other. Two football states being able to play one another on an October night."

—Nick Mangold, Buckeyes center

Nabil K. Mark/Centre Daily Times

Maybe it's because they haven't defeated Michigan in nine years, or even played the Wolverines in nearly three. Maybe it's because that Land Grant Trophy just doesn't do it for them. Something gets the Nittany Lions geared up for the Buckeyes like no other game.

"I think a lot of us view it as our No. 1 rival because we always play them close, whether we have a weak team or a good team," said Penn State safety Chris Harrell, one of 21 seniors who will get one final shot at defeating the Buckeyes. "Mainly because we have such large traditions that are going up against each other."

Maybe that's it. The tradition. Memories of Woody Hayes and Eddie George, of Curtis Enis and Zack Mills.

"It's two states going after each other," said Buckeyes center Nick Mangold. "Two football states being able to play one another on an October night."

Because behind the ESPN crews and the power rankings and whether or not a team is "back" is an actual football game. Two teams, 60 minutes, one pigskin.

"That's what college football's supposed to be about," said Penn State quarterback Michael Robinson.

It is. And, whether the Nittany Lions win or lose, it's here in Happy Valley this weekend. *GameDay* or not.

RIGHT: **Fred Wilson (left) and Charlie Leckner play cribbage before a Penn State football game.**
Craig Houtz/Centre Daily Times

PENN STATE UPSETS NO. 6 OHIO STATE

BY JEFF RICE

They met at about the 35-yard line, the respective leaders of Penn State's offense and defense, and embraced, knowing the win was simply the next installment of their master plan but recognizing its significance all the same. The giddy mob of players and students and cameramen swarmed around Michael Robinson and Paul Posluszny, who lived in memorable fashion the stories of two different halves that added up to the Nittany Lions' 17-10 defeat of No. 6 Ohio State.

Robinson led Penn State (6-0, 3-0 Big Ten) to an early 14-3 lead against one of the nation's top defenses before Posluszny and his charges showed the Nittany Lions, the conference's lone unbeaten after Wisconsin's loss at Northwestern, have a defense that deserves just as much attention.

The 109,839 in Beaver Stadium stayed until the end, shaking the stadium to its core from Derrick Williams' second-quarter touchdown jaunt until Tamba Hali separated Buckeyes quarterback Troy Smith from the football and Scott Paxson recovered it with 81 seconds to play.

For Penn State coach Joe Paterno, who won his eighth straight game and the 349th of his career, it was a good, tough win over a good, tough team, and little more.

"We got one more touchdown than they did," Paterno said, reminding the assembled media that his team visits Michigan next week. "But I thought it was a heck of a football game."

For the Buckeyes (3-2, 1-1), perennial Big Ten title contenders, it was the latest in a long line of will-testers, a prime-time bout with a tough, balanced squad in a hostile environment.

But for the Nittany Lions, it represented a shot at something bigger, a chance to silence what critics remained even after a 5-0 start and prove themselves as, at the very least, legitimate contenders for the Big Ten title.

"We love when people doubt us," said cornerback Alan Zemaitis. "We play for ourselves and the fans that we have here—we don't play for nobody else."

Penn State, which defeated the Buckeyes for just the second time in five seasons but for the fifth time in the last seven in Beaver Stadium, never trailed and was turnover-free for the second straight week.

OPPOSITE PAGE: **Tamba Hali sends Ohio State quarterback Troy Smith head over heels late in the game. Smith was sacked five times.**
Jason Malmont/Centre Daily Times

But there was a sense, particularly in the second half, that the Nittany Lions were getting sucked in to the same old Ohio State trap. They increased their lead to a touchdown early in the third quarter but the Buckeyes, so accustomed to pulling out close games, remained frighteningly calm, sticking to their game plan and daring Penn State to put them away. A.J. Hawk and the gritty Buckeyes defense got nastier as the night wore on and kept their erratic offense in the game. Penn State had just 22 net yards over the final 23 minutes.

It became evident that Penn State's defense was going to have to win this one.

And it did.

"They just played tremendous," said wide receiver Deon Butler. "Time after time they stepped up to the call. Other teams get all the publicity about their defense, but our guys step up every time they need to."

Penn State's offense stepped up just enough early on.

The teams traded punts and possessions like heavyweights feeling each other out during the first few possessions, the Buckeyes drawing first blood.

After an 11-yard punt from Jeremy Kapinos, the Buckeyes drove 44 yards in 12 plays to the Penn State 13, where Josh Huston kicked a 30-yard field goal to put Ohio State ahead 3-0 with 6:41 remaining in the first quarter.

Seven minutes later, the Nittany Lions found the burst that would clinch the game, but they couldn't have known it then.

A 25-yard burst from tailback Tony Hunt (16 carries, 64 yards) drove the Nittany Lions deep into Buckeyes territory, while Robinson, who evaded heavy pressure from the Ohio State front seven all night, scrambled 16 yards to the Buckeyes 13-yard line.

OPPOSITE PAGE: **Senior safety Calvin Lowry goes airborne after intercepting the ball and taking it to the two-yard line. Michael Robinson scored on a quarterback keeper three plays later.**
Nabil K. Mark/Centre Daily Times

	1st	2nd	3rd	4th	Final
Ohio State	3	7	0	0	10
Penn State	0	14	3	0	17

Scoring Summary
OSU—Huston 30-yard field goal, 12 plays, 44 yards in 5:40
PSU—Williams 13-yard run (Kelly kick), nine plays, 74 yards in 4:27
PSU—Robinson 1-yard run (Kelly kick), three plays, two yards in 1:25
OSU—Smith 10-yard run (Huston kick), 14 plays, 81 yards in 7:13
PSU—Kelly 41-yard field goal, 10 plays, 45 yards in 3:45

Team Statistics

Category	OSU	PSU
First Downs	16	11
Rushes-Yards (Net)	40-91	37-117
Passing Yards (Net)	139	78
Passes Att-Comp-Int	25-13-1	20-11-0
Total Offense Plays-Yards	65-230	57-195
Punt Returns-Yards	2-5	1-3
Kickoff Returns-Yards	4-59	2-18
Punts (Number-Avg)	6-43.7	7-34.6
Fumbles-Lost	3-1	1-0
Penalties-Yards	4-25	5-29
Possession Time	31:42	28:18
Sacks By (Number-Yards)	0-0	5-34

Individual Statistics
Rushing: **Ohio State**-Pittman 15-58; Smith 19-15; Schnittker 4-13; Ginn 2-5.
Penn State-Hunt 16-64; Robinson 14-52; Williams 4-10; Team 3-(-9).

Passing: **Ohio State**-Smith 13-25-1-139.
Penn State-Robinson 11-20-0-78.

Receiving: **Ohio State**-Holmes 4-41; Ginn 3-40; Hamby 2-24; Pittman 2-20; White 1-11; Hall 1-3.
Penn State-Norwood 5-36; Butler 3-30; Williams 1-11; Snow 1-7; King 1-(-6).

Interceptions: **Ohio State**-None.
Penn State-Lowry 1-36.

Sacks (Unassisted-Assisted): **Ohio State**-None.
Penn State-Hali 1-1; Connor 1-0; Rice 0-1; Posluszny 1-0; Alford 1-0.

Tackles (Unassisted-Assisted): **Ohio State**-Hawk 5-4; Schlegel 4-5; Patterson 3-2; Whitner 4-0; Salley 4-0; Carpenter 2-2; Youboty 2-2; Jenkins 3-0; Everett 2-1; Green 1-2; Harley 2-0.
Penn State-Posluszny 6-8; Harrell 6-6; Connor 5-7; Lowry 3-4; Hali 2-5; Rice 1-5; Zemaitis 3-1; Alford 1-3; Sales 1-2; T. Shaw 0-3; King 2-0; Paxson 2-0; Kilmer 1-1.

Williams, who had a mostly quiet evening, took a pitch from Robinson, got a great clear-out block from right tackle Andrew Richardson, squeaked past a lunging A.J. Hawk and darted 13 yards into the end zone—directly in front of the Ohio State contingent of fans—and the Nittany Lions led 7-3.

Then, as "Zombie Nation" blared from the loudspeakers, Beaver Stadium began to rumble. Three plays later, Smith was intercepted by Calvin

ABOVE: **Penn State tailback Tony Hunt breaks Bobby Carpenter's tackle for a long gain in the first half. Hunt led all rushers with 64 yards.** *Nabil K. Mark/Centre Daily Times*

Lowry, who returned the ball 36 yards to the Ohio State two-yard line. Three plays after that, Robinson took it in on an option keeper.

Penn State 14, Ohio State 3. Seven minutes and 55 seconds remained in the second quarter.

The Buckeyes were not about to fold as easily as Minnesota had here the week before in a 44-14 loss. A pair of Smith completions to tight end Ryan Hamby got the Buckeyes into Penn State territory, where Tressel returned to the ground game. Smith, Antonio Pittman and fullback Brandon Schnittker took turns churning Ohio State to the 10 before Smith bulled his way into the end zone, stretching the ball across the goal line with 33 seconds left in the half to pull the Buckeyes within four.

But that was it for Smith and Ohio State, which never got speedy receiver Ted Ginn (three catches, 40 yards) going and never really threatened in the

second half, despite forcing four straight three-and-outs by the Nittany Lions.

The Penn State pass rush, led by Tamba Hali, increased its pressure on Smith, while Posluszny, who led all defenders with 14 tackles, was there at every turn.

"I don't think you can play any better football than he played today," Paterno said.

Robinson, meanwhile, led Penn State to its lowest yardage total (195 of the season), but was at his best with Hawk or another Buckeye directly in his face, avoiding the rush for big scrambles or clutch passes when it looked as though he was in for a hefty loss.

"Quarterbacks have a mental clock," said Robinson, who rushed for 52 yards on 14 carries and completed 11-of-20 passes for 78 yards. "You feel some things coming, you start shuffling, you shuffle once or twice, you gotta go. God has blessed me with the legs and the ability to get away from things like that."

Kevin Kelly's 41-yard field goal on Penn State's opening drive of the half increased the lead to 17-10 with 11:10 remaining in the third. Then both offenses shut down. The Buckeyes could do little with the football but the Nittany Lions kept giving them chances.

"I was scared to death the whole time," Paterno admitted with a smile. "One play."

But the Buckeyes never got that play from Ginn, or from his brash fellow wideout Santonio Holmes. Pittman was held to 58 yards rushing and the Buckeyes only got into Penn State territory once in the fourth quarter. The game was the defense's to win or lose, and Penn State's came through—narrowly.

"I ain't satisfied until all the time is off the clock," Zemaitis said.

When the final seconds had ticked off, and fans began planning for Ann Arbor and a bowl (the Nittany Lions' sixth win made them postseason-eligible), its leaders allowed themselves a brief moment, a few seconds to smile before getting back to work.

This night, on this grand stage, they had both earned it.

ABOVE: **Senior defensive tackle Scott Paxson celebrates after recovering Ohio State quarterback Troy Smith's fourth-quarter fumble.**
Craig Houtz/Centre Daily Times

PENN STATE 0
17 <
DOWN TO GO
4TH 20

W
W

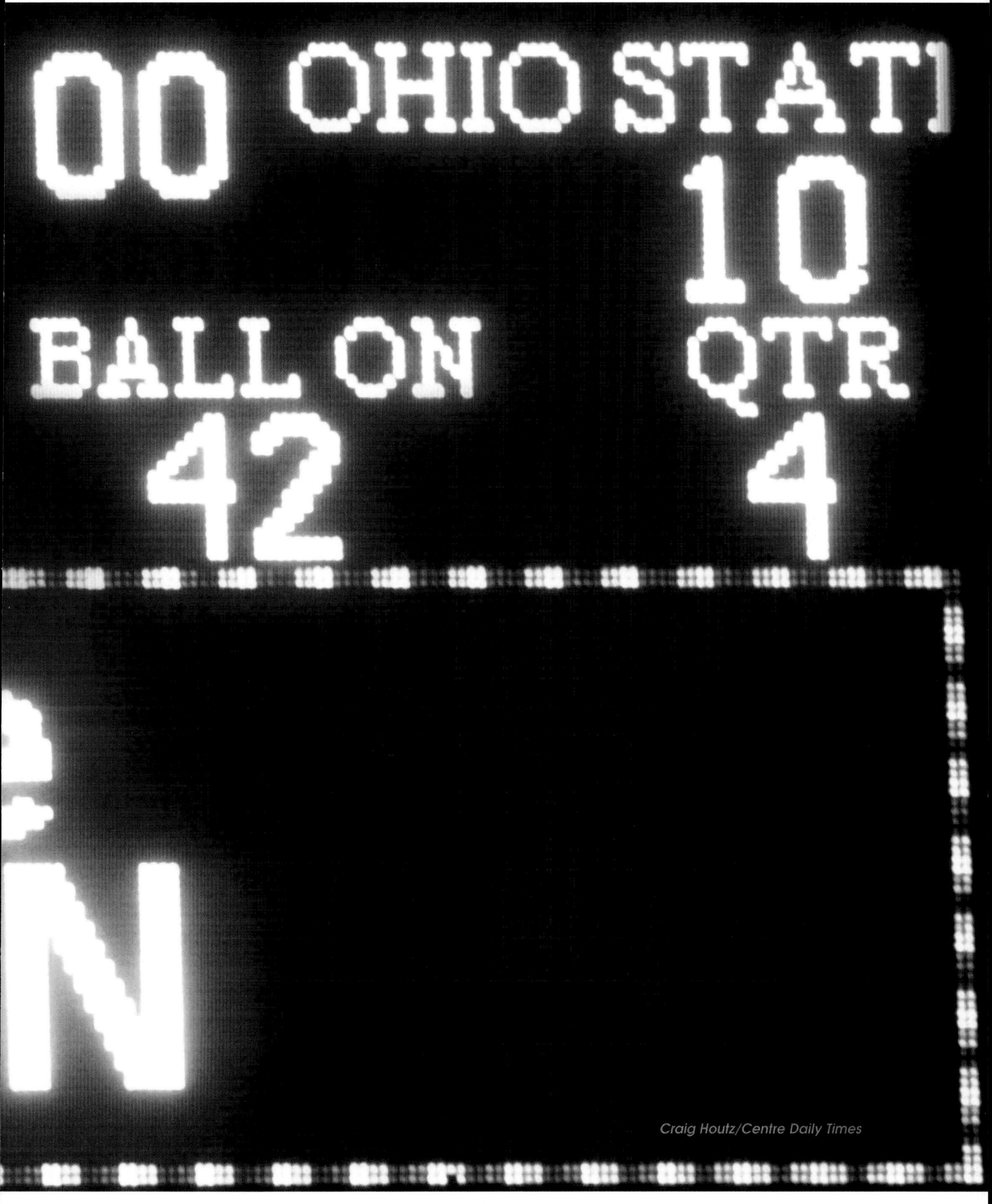

00 OHIO STATI
10
BALL ON
42
QTR
4
N

Craig Houtz/Centre Daily Times

THIS GAME LINES UP WITH OTHER GREAT WINS

BY RON BRACKEN

Go ahead, make a list of the great football games that have been played in Beaver Stadium. Go back to 1967 when unbeaten, third-ranked North Carolina State rolled into town wearing white shoes and great ambitions and left on the short end of a 13-8 defeat that launched Penn State onto the national stage.

Go back to 1982 when Nebraska and Penn State played a game for the ages under the lights and the Nittany Lions beat the Huskers on their way to their first national championship.

Or, in more recent history, go back to 2001 when the Nittany Lions, led by fuzzy-cheeked freshman Zack Mills knocked off Ohio State and gave Joe Paterno his 324th win, moving him past Bear Bryant.

And now you can add the 17-10 triumph over sixth-ranked Ohio State in front of 109,839 fans to any list of the greatest games ever played in the big steel bowl.

It lived up to the hype, matched the enthusiasm of the fans with performance on the field. And when it was all over there were celebrations all the way from Monroeville to Phoenixville to Paternoville. These Nittany Lions, who have lived with the bitter taste of losing are now sipping the heady wine of being 6-0 and bowl eligible.

If last week's pasting of Minnesota was the statement game they said it was, this one was a proclamation that they are back in the territory their predecessors took for granted.

But it wasn't until Tamba Hali blindsided Troy Smith, causing him to fumble the football and teammate Scott Paxson scooped up the loose ball that Penn State was virtually guaranteed of the victory. Then a Vesuvius of emotion erupted from the stands and along the sidelines. Ohio State's last chance had vaporized in the moist October night.

"He was in my sights and I thought he was going to throw the ball," said Hali, who roared in from the right side. "He kept the ball too long so I changed my speed and tried to go all out. I just wanted to go hit him so he couldn't throw the ball. It felt good when I hit him and Paxson scooped up the ball. It's fun chasing a quarterback like that and getting to him."

Hali said the crowd served as a motivator for him throughout the game.

"That crowd is the reason I came to Penn State," he said. "They support us every time. So when you get on the field you can't do anything but go all out. Coach [Larry] Johnson said that this game wasn't going to be won in the first quarter, second quarter or third quarter. He said it was going to be won in the fourth quarter and we just had to keep on throwing punches."

Once he delivered what proved to be the knockout punch to Smith at the Ohio State 48 with 2:16 left in the game it was clear that this night belonged to Penn State, lock, stock and first place in the Big Ten standings.

It was especially sweet for safety Chris Harrell, a native of Euclid, Ohio.

"It's really hard to explain how I feel right now," he said, the smile splitting his face saying what he couldn't find the words to express. "This is the first time in five years that we felt confident on the sidelines, that we were comfortable and not

OPPOSITE PAGE: **Penn State quarterback Michael Richardson celebrates the 17-10 upset win over the Buckeyes with the student section.**
Craig Houtz/Centre Daily Times

nervous. It's the first time we could go out there and be confident that the man next to you was going to do his job.

"This was a chance for us to prove we belonged on the national stage. They were doing a lot of trash talking about how they were going to shut us down. We wanted to show people across the country that we could stop the big plays.

"We took offense that people were saying that our defense wasn't any good, that their linebackers were better, how they had the better secondary. Now we're 6-0 and I definitely think we belong in the top 10. I think that we proved we can play with just about anybody."

Paterno has presided over all of the great victories Penn State has registered in the past half century or so. He knows how temporary they are when they come in the midst of a season when the next game suddenly becomes the biggest on the schedule. Last night's win loses all of its luster if his team goes to Ann Arbor and falls short against Michigan.

But on this night, after an intense week of preparation for a game so full of meaning, he was at least able to smile and savor the victory, all the while keeping it in perspective.

"We beat a good football team," he said, sipping from a bottle of water. "I don't want to get carried away over one win. I've tried to play it down, but people tried to make this the game. I think we have a good football team but we can get better. This was a heck of a football game and we won. I'm pleased, obviously, but we have to realize this isn't the end of the road for this team."

Not even close. Five regular-season games remain for the Nittany Lions. Then there will be a postseason game for the first time since 2002.

What this win did was open all kinds of possibilities as to where this team will be spending the latter part of December.

What it did was finally silence the doubters who wondered how the freshmen would fare against a quality defense, how the offensive line would deal with the savvy linebacking trio Ohio State trotted out, how Michael Robinson would handle the pressure of his first start in the suffocating pressure of a game of this magnitude.

And all of the question marks were turned into exclamation points. The Nittany Lions played a nearly perfect game. They were turnover free, had only five penalties for 29 yards and allowed the Buckeyes to convert only six of 15 third-down attempts.

It was exactly the type of game Paterno has built a career on—playing great defense, winning the kicking game and scoring just enough points to win. The special teams were especially crucial, keeping Ted Ginn and Santonio Holmes contained to 64 yards combined on punts and kickoff returns.

"[Jeremy] Kapinos didn't kick for distance but he gave us a chance to cover," Paterno said. "We worked hard on that area. And when you can tie that in with good defense then you've got a shot in any game you play if you don't turn it over."

That's a formula that's worked since the days of leather helmets and drop kicks.

This night it was as effective as penicillin as the Nittany Lions lengthened their list of landmark victories by one.

OPPOSITE PAGE: **Derrick Williams celebrates after the first touchdown against Ohio State.**
Nabil K. Mark/Centre Daily Times

31 PAUL POSLUSZNY

**BIRTHDATE: 10/10/84 BIRTHPLACE: BUTLER, PA HIGH SCHOOL: HOPEWELL (ALIQUIPPA, PA)
MAJOR: FINANCE POSITION: LINEBACKER HEIGHT: 6'2" WEIGHT: 229 LBS**

It's the mark of a warrior, as sure to identify Paul Posluszny as a football player as if he'd shown up in class wearing his helmet.

Wrestlers have cauliflower ears, boxers have flattened noses. Football players have a divot on the bridge of their nose during the season that becomes a scar once their career's done.

It comes from the way they're taught to tackle, sticking their face in the opponent's numbers, seeing what they hit.

"It's a classic football injury," said the Penn State junior tri-captain who is emerging as a classic linebacker in the mold of the great ones who have preceded him. "It rips open every Saturday. It won't go away until after the bowl game."

Yes, he did say bowl game. In years past, it was a given that Penn State would be playing in the shadows of palm trees or cacti. But not the recent past, not in Posluszny's time.

Now, because of Poszluszny and the rest of the Penn State defense, the Nittany Lions are one game away from being bowl eligible. As bright and shiny as the offense has been up to now, the ultimate success and failure of this team rests on the shoulder pads of the defense.

And the defense is led by Posluszny, who has been named the Big Ten Defensive Player of the Week the past two weeks. He's the ignitor, roaming sideline to sideline looking for the man with the football and his intentions are bad. He leads the team in tackles with 57, 33 of them solo, from his outside linebacker spot.

"One thing coach [Ron] Vanderlinden talks about all the time is that we have to go all out on every play, trying to get to the football," Posluszny said. "He says our attitude has to be 'If you don't make the play, who's going to?' So each of us tries to get to the ball every time.

"I won't lie, I get tired all of the time. But to be one of the best you can't be one of the best some of the time, you have to go all out every play. That's what the great ones do."

A lot of the great ones at Penn State have worn No. 31, including Shane Conlan, the anchor of the 1986 national championship team whose style Posluszny most closely resembles.

Posluszny wound up with the number at the suggestion of equipment manager Brad Caldwell, who was around when Conlan was playing.

"I wore No. 39 my freshman year but [fullback] Paul Jefferson redshirted that year and when he came back he got his number back," Posluszny explained. "Spider [Caldwell] said that 31 was available and it would be a good number for me because it has a lot of tradition. Then I found out all of the guys who wore it (including Andre Collins and Mac Morrison) and I saw how special it really was.

"I just want to do things the right way, play like those guys did. I want to be part of the tradition, to uphold the tradition. It's a disservice to them if we do anything less."

Against Ohio State, great linebackers will be as common as hash marks. Penn State will throw out Posluszny, Dan Connor and Tim Shaw. Ohio State will counter with A.J. Hawk, Bobby Carpenter and Anthony Schlegel, a unit that is considered the best in college football this year.

"This game will be in prime time so a lot of people will be watching. It gives us a shot at showing we can be up there too, that we've got good linebackers too. We want to show everyone how good we are, how good we can be."

Posluszny gave everyone a glimpse of his own considerable abilities when he smacked down Minnesota's Gary Russell at the one-yard line early in the fourth quarter. Russell had tried to leap over the Penn State defense but Posluszny met him at the apex of his leap above the goal line and drove him back. It was a highlight film play even though, in the overall scheme of things, it meant little since the Gophers scored on the next play to make it 37-14.

But it added to the burgeoning image of Posluszny as an outstanding linebacker.

"We felt it would be a run," he said. "We knew that on the goal line they like to run the power play. I saw their running back take a step forward, our defensive line cut everyone down and it (leaping) just seemed like the right thing to do. My instinct said to go airborne and meet the running back and it worked out for the best.

"Anytime you make a play like that you don't hear anything while the play is going on but then you hear the crowd. That's why we play football. For a linebacker to make a big hit like that, it's definitely a fun time. At this level that is certainly my favorite play."

It's the kind of play his defensive teammates have come to expect from the six-foot-two, 229-pound finance major from Aliquippa.

"I know I can depend on him having my back, depend on him to get the play calls, make sure our defense is set right," said defensive end Matthew Rice.

Posluszny is an intense competitor as well, even if it's something as simple as being first in conditioning runs in the summer. That too, is part of the Posluszny personna that has its roots in his childhood battles with his older brother, Stan, who played baseball at West Virginia.

It was during this past summer when incoming freshman Sean Lee joined Posluszny and some of the upperclassmen for a workout. Part of the regimen was 10 300-yard runs. Posluszny won the first nine but Lee edged him in the 10th one. That went over like a dropped interception.

"I guess on the 10th one he had a little bit more energy and he beat me," Posluszny said. "I was startled. I was disappointed in myself but I

was also glad for him because he showed he's a competitor."

Posluszny carries a 3.68 GPA—"I need to do well in class to keep my mom happy," he said—and if playing on Sunday afternoons is not in his future he plans to join the military.

"I'd like to join the Navy, I'd like to fly, go to OCS and be an officer. I'd like to do my part. I don't know if it's feasible for me to fly but if I can't I'd go with something else."

But there are a lot of tackles to be made, a lot of goal-line stands between now and then. There is also the matter of completing his body of work as a linebacker at Linebacker U.

"I'd like to think I'm a smart player," he said, "that I'm someone who has instincts and makes the right decisions. I guess I'd like to be considered as someone who is tough and aggressive."

Without those traits he wouldn't be a linebacker, wouldn't have the battle scars that come with the position.

"He's a warrior, man," Rice said. "Poz, in a few words, is a relentless warrior."

By Ron Bracken

Craig Houtz/Centre Daily Times

PENN STATE'S BIG WIN MAKES SOME 'BELIEVERS'

BY WALT MOODY

The Monkees sang in one of their biggest hits, "Then I saw her face, now I'm a believer."

Excuse the '60s music reference, but if we saw the true face of the Penn State football team against Ohio State, then there are quite a few more believers that big-time college football has been revived in Happy Valley.

The Nittany Lions' 17-10 triumph may not have been a masterpiece for the eyes, but it showcased the willingness of a team to do what was necessary to win a big game—play great defense and don't turn the ball over.

That hasn't happened much over the previous five seasons, but the Nittany Lions have done it twice on consecutive Saturdays against then-No. 18 Minnesota (a 44-14 triumph) and against the No. 6 Buckeyes.

The result is a building clamor from Nittany Nation proclaiming, "We're back."

According to Ohio State coach Jim Tressel, Penn State never left. The hard-nosed defense is the same, but he sees the big difference this season is the No. 12 of Michael Robinson lining up behind the center.

"They were never gone," Tressel said after his team dropped to 3-2. "You saw what their defense did a year ago. Offensively, I thought they struggled a year ago because they had [Zack] Mills part of the time and they had Robinson part of the time. They were different guys and it was hard to get a real flow."

Robinson's play certainly has been the biggest difference in the Nittany Lions' rise to No. 8 in the Associated Press rankings.

After struggling holding onto the ball (four fumbles lost, six interceptions) in the first four games, Robinson has not given the ball away.

While his throws always may not be the most accurate (24 for 52 in the last two games), Robinson is missing in the right spots where no defensive back has a shot at making a momentum-changing play.

He's also reading defenses better, a fact that wasn't lost on the Buckeyes. Ohio State came with several blitzes off the corners and Robinson routinely found the receiver who drew soft man-to-man coverage.

"He was doing a good job of recognizing it," Ohio State linebacker Bobby Carpenter said of the blitzes. "He was throwing it out there and they were making plays."

Robinson also is "making plays" with his feet. The Buckeyes, who entered the game with a conference-leading 16 sacks, had none against the Nittany Lions thanks to Robinson. On multiple occasions, Robinson was able to slip a tackle or break an arm tackle to avoid the sack. He also burned Ohio State with a 16-yard scramble on Penn State's first touchdown march.

"We knew coming in that he has a lot of talent," said Buckeyes linebacker A.J. Hawk, who was frustrated with his team's tackling despite giving up just 195 total yards to the Nittany Lions. "He does things like that. He eludes pressure and he gives himself time and then when he needs to he tucks it and runs."

Running is where Robinson is the most dangerous. He's quick and strong as he proved in

ABOVE: **This season has given all Nittany Lions fans something to cheer about.** *Craig Houtz/Centre Daily Times*

bowling over a tackler at the goal line for the Nittany Lions' second touchdown.

It was a solid performance, especially when compared to his Ohio State counterpart Troy Smith, who was supposed to be the more versatile of the two. The Buckeyes quarterback threw a game-changing interception that led to a score and a 14-3 Nittany Lions lead and fumbled on Ohio State's last-gasp drive with less than two minutes remaining.

Smith also had receivers Santonio Holmes and Ted Ginn Jr., jumping up and down in frustration on several occasions when he threw into coverage when they were open.

Part of Smith's problem was that to deal with Penn State's pass rush (five sacks) and when he scrambled he ran smack into Paul Posluszny (14 tackles) and Dan Connor (12 tackles).

"We got behind the count and it allowed them to pin their ears back," Tressel said. "They did a good job with that."

The defense did such a good job that Paterno let the air out of the ball midway through the third quarter to make sure the Buckeyes and Smith had to beat his defense.

The Nittany Lions offense went three-and-out on every drive in the final quarter, but it didn't matter because the defense stymied the Buckeyes.

"They were very simple and executed very well," Tressel said of the Nittany Lions. "They didn't play any fancy coverages. They played three-deep and they played two-deep and occasionally blitzed and played man. I just thought that they executed well.

"Every play is designed to work and every defense is designed to go against every play. It's just a matter of who executes and they won."

The Nittany Lions (6-0) will need the same kind of execution this week against struggling Michigan (3-3) in the "Big House." Penn State has lost six straight to the Wolverines, who won the last meeting 27-24 in overtime in 2002.

A big win on the road is all that is lacking on Penn State's resume this season. With one, they'll make more believers.

Tressel is one.

"I think ... that they've decided who they are and what they're going to do and everyone is a year older that has been playing for quite some time," he said. "They're a good football team."

"They were very simple and executed very well. They didn't play any fancy coverages. They played three deep and they played two deep and occasionally blitzed and played man. I just thought that they executed well.

— Jim Tressel, Ohio State coach

LEFT: **This Penn State team is winning over more fans as it adds to the win column.**
Nabil K. Mark/Centre Daily Times

HEARTBREAKER IN ANN ARBOR

BY JEFF RICE

To the players in white, the walk up a slight incline through the tunnel to the locker room seemed endless.

Matthew Rice trudged to the door, one tired step at a time. Five feet across the hall, the blue-jerseyed players of Michigan ran through their door bouncing and hollering. The Penn State defensive end looked over for just a second, knowing that if not for one play, his locker room would have the opposite feeling.

Which is all it came down to in Michigan Stadium—one second, one play. Answering every shot by the Nittany Lions in a furious fourth quarter with one of its own, Michigan defeated No. 8 Penn State 27-25 on a 10-yard touchdown pass from Chad Henne to Mario Manningham as time expired.

The Nittany Lions (6-1, 3-1 Big Ten) had taken a 25-21 lead on a three-yard touchdown run by quarterback Michael Robinson with 53 seconds to play before the Wolverines (4-3, 2-2), taking over at the 47 after a sensational 41-yard kickoff return by Steve Breaston, drove 53 yards in eight plays for the

RIGHT: Running back Tony Hunt carries the ball against Michigan. Hunt led Penn State in rushing yards with 102, but did not score in the game.
Tom Pidgeon/Getty Images

game-winning score, ending a classic game as 111,249 became delirious.

One second remained on the game clock when Henne dropped back on fourth-and-goal from the 10-yard line. Breaston was the first read for the Wyomissing native, who threw for 135 yards and two touchdowns in the second half, both to Manningham. The freshman wideout split Penn State defenders Alan Zemaitis and Calvin Lowry on a slant and Henne hit him in the back of the end zone.

"I think he is always ready to make that kind of play," Henne said.

Penn State head coach Joe Paterno didn't make his players available to the media after the Nittany Lions' last visit to Ann Arbor, a 27-24 overtime loss in 2002, and didn't see the need to either.

"I just wanna get them on the bus, get to the airport and go home, so we can start thinking about next week instead of having them moan about what happened," Paterno said. "You ask them the same questions you ask me. They don't feel like talking."

Paterno, who saw his team lose its seventh straight to Michigan, didn't have much to say about the two seconds the officials put back on the clock on Michigan's final drive, either.

A completion from Henne to Carl Tabb near the left sideline got the Wolverines to the Penn State 32-yard line, but Tabb couldn't get out-of-bounds before being tackled by Justin King. The Wolverines called timeout with 28 seconds left. After some deliberation, the officials put two seconds back on the clock. Paterno said he did not receive an explanation for the added time.

"What can I do?" he said later. "There's nothing I can do about it."

	1st	2nd	3rd	4th	Final
Penn State	0	0	3	22	25
Michigan	0	3	7	17	27

Scoring Summary
MICH—Rivas 35-yard field goal, seven plays, 53 yards in 2:38
MICH—Hart 2-yard run (Rivas kick), 10 plays, 70 yards in 3:50
PSU—Kelly 25-yard field goal, seven plays, 67 yards in 2:42
PSU Robinson 4-yard run (Kelly kick), four plays, 63 yards in 1:08
PSU—Zemaitis 35-yard fumble return (Kelly rush)
MICH—Manningham 33-yard pass from Henne (Hart rush), five plays, 55 yards in 2:07
MICH—Rivas 47-yard field goal, nine plays, 28 yards in 3:30
PSU—Robinson 3-yard run (Kelly kick), 13 plays, 81 yards in 1:53
MICH—Manningham 10-yard pass from Henne, eight plays, 53 yards in 0:53

Team Statistics
Category	PSU	MICH
First Downs	20	21
Rushes-Yards (Net)	38-181	39-163
Passing Yards (Net)	239	212
Passes Att-Comp-Int	34-19-1	36-21-0
Total Offense Plays-Yards	72-420	75-375
Punt Returns-Yards	1-11	2-28
Kickoff Returns-Yards	3-37	5-136
Punts (Number-Avg)	4-47.0	6-40.7
Fumbles-Lost	2-1	1-1
Penalties-Yards	6-35	5-49
Possession Time	30:49	29:11
Sacks By (Number-Yards)	3-14	1-8

Individual Statistics
Rushing: Penn State-Hunt 14-102; Robinson 17-67; Williams 3-8; King 1-5; Scott 1-2; Snow 1-(-1); Team 1-(-2).
Michigan-Hart 23-108; Bass 2-26; Grady 5-25; Breaston 2-3; Tabb 1-3; Henne 6-(-2).

Passing: Penn State-Robinson 19-34-1-239.
Michigan-Henne 21-36-0-212.

Receiving: Penn State-Williams 6-59; Norwood 4-63; Golden 3-74; Smolko 2-24; Hunt 2-0; Kilmer 1-13; Butler 1-6.
Michigan-Avant 8-75; Hart 4-40; Manningham 3-49; Ecker 3-29; Breaston 1-10; Massaquoi, 1-5; Tabb 1-4.

Interceptions: Penn State-None.
Michigan-Hall 1-14.

Sacks (Unassisted-Assisted): Penn State-Hali 1-0; Paxson 1-0; Alford 1-0.
Michigan-Woodley 1-0.

Tackles (Unassisted-Assisted): Penn State-Posluszny 8-3; Harrell 7-3; Hali 6-3; Connor 6-3; Zemaitis 7-0; King 5-1; Paxson 3-3; Alford 3-3; Lowry 4-1; Kilmer 3-0; Rice 1-2; Smith 2-0; T. Shaw 1-1.
Michigan-Mason 7-3; Harris 7-3; Adams 8-0; Burgess 7-1; Woodley 6-2; Hall 6-1; Trent 3-0; Watson 2-1; Branch 1-2; Massey 2-0.

OPPOSITE PAGE: **Linebacker Paul Posluszny (31) takes down Michigan running back Kevin Grady. Posluszny led Penn State with eight tackles.** *Tom Pidgeon/Getty Images*

The pass before, a 17-yard connection from Henne to Jason Avant, was near the opposite sideline. Television replays showed Avant's heel landed out-of-bounds, but the Wolverines got the next play off before the officials could review it.

The last two possessions were emblematic of the greatest fourth quarter in the all-time series, which the Wolverines now lead 8-3. The teams combined for 13 points in the first 48 minutes and four seconds and 39 points in the final 11:56.

"I have had a number of wild games in the past few years," said Michigan head coach Lloyd Carr, who has watched each of his team's four conference games this season be decided in the final minute or overtime. "But I have never had a wilder game than this one."

The fourth began unassumingly enough, with Michigan, leading 10-3 and driving 11 yards to its own 29-yard line before punting. Then the Nittany Lions' Tony Hunt (14 rushes, 102 yards), who had been bottled up most of the afternoon, ripped off a 61-yard run to the Michigan two-yard line, and Robinson took a quarterback draw into the end zone from four yards out two plays later. Kevin Kelly's extra point tied the game at 10-10.

On the very next play from scrimmage, Penn State cornerback Alan Zemaitis stood Henne up with a savage hit, stripped the ball and trotted 35 yards to paydirt before a stunned Wolverines crowd. Holder Jason Ganter bobbled the extra-point snap, but the five-foot-seven Kelly picked it up and took it in for two points himself.

Michigan, though, struck right back, Henne finding Manningham on a pretty 33-yard spiral just over the head of King. Hart's two-point conversion run tied the score, and Michigan took a 21-18 lead six minutes later on a 47-yard field goal from Garrett Rivas.

Robinson (19 of 34, 239 yards, one interception), drove the Nittany Lions 81 yards in 13 plays, all without top threat Derrick Williams, who sustained an unspecified injury to his left arm on the kickoff return and did not return. Penn State

spokesman Jeff Nelson said Williams would be evaluated by team doctors back in State College.

The senior quarterback, who also ran 17 times for 67 yards, picked up a first down on fourth-and-seven with a nine-yard run and drove Penn State to the Michigan 15. A pass interference call on Leon Hall against Terrell Golden put the ball at the three-yard line, and Robinson bulled his way into the end zone on a quarterback draw.

Fifty-three seconds, however, remained.

Paterno said afterward he was kicking himself for kicking to Breaston, who piled up 156 return yards Saturday.

"If there's just a little skinny place for him," marveled Henne, "he'll hit that hole."

Penn State looked very much the better team early on but couldn't come up with the points to prove it. Kelly missed a field goal in each quarter and Robinson lost a fumble.

Michigan had also been misfiring offensively, picking up just two first downs and 42 total yards in the first quarter, but found a spark in freshman wideout Antonio Bass. Lining up at quarterback on Michigan's third drive of the game, Bass took a shotgun snap and raced 23 yards to the Penn State 44. Henne hit Jason Avant for 21 yards on the next play, and three plays later Rivas hit a 35-yard field goal with 4:34 left in the half.

Robinson then led the Nittany Lions to the Michigan 49 before David Harris jarred the ball from his grasp after a 10-yard run and Brandon Harrison recovered. Penn State called timeout in the hopes the officials would review the play, and they did, but the initial ruling was upheld. It was Penn State's first turnover in 11 quarters.

"The defenses on both sides of the field played so well in the first half that you can get into a mindset that it is going to be that way for the rest of the game," Carr said.

Michigan opened the second half with a 10-play, 70-yard drive capped off with a two-yard touchdown run from Hart (23 carries, 108 yards) to take a 10-0 lead. A wild fumbled-snap, scrambling pass from Robinson to Golden went for 56 yards to set up Kelly's 25-yard field goal with 10 seconds left before the third quarter ended and the madness began.

The Wolverines, who had struggled to a 3-3 start, particularly in Big Ten play, avoided falling below .500 in October for the first time since 1967 and moved within a game of first-place in the wide-open Big Ten standings.

"A victory like this just puts us back in the place we want to be," Henne said.

Penn State, which fell into a share of first place in the conference with 5-1, 3-1 Wisconsin, visits Illinois on October 22.

"We've played two great football games, three really," Paterno said. "These kids have hung in there. I'm proud of them. I don't know what else I could say. I'm proud of them; I'm disappointed for them."

RIGHT: **Penn State quarterback Michael Robinson carries the ball against Michigan. Robinson ran for two touchdowns in the game.**
Tom Pidgeon/Getty Images

Penn State head coach Joe Paterno greets Michigan head coach Lloyd Carr before the start of the game at Michigan Stadium.
Tom Pidgeon/Getty Images

NITTANY LIONS CAN'T HANG THEIR HEADS

BY WALT MOODY

One second. One play.

That's what stands between Penn State's grandest of dreams and what is the reality of a Big Ten Conference chock full of teams that you can throw a blanket over.

This epic 27-25 loss to Michigan likely will quell the talk of the Rose Bowl, but there's a lot left on the line for this football team.

The Nittany Lions are still among the five teams (Wisconsin, Ohio State, Northwestern and Iowa) with one conference loss, and their destiny likely is still in their own hands. Having beaten Ohio State and Northwestern and having Wisconsin still on the schedule, the Nittany Lions can win out and still have the opportunity to take home the trophy and a Bowl Championship Series bid. Iowa still faces Michigan, Northwestern, Wisconsin and Minnesota.

So instead of skulking off into the darkness without a word (as they've done the past two times in the "Big House" thanks to their coach's wishes), the Nittany Lions should leave with their heads held high.

While the 17-10 win over Ohio State may have been the first big step in the program's revival, this loss may have cemented the fact that the Nittany Lions are a legitimate force again.

In a frenetic track meet of a fourth quarter, Penn State proved that it could rally from a pair of deficits and take the lead under the most hostile of circumstances. Twice in the final quarter the offense proved it could drive and find the end zone.

The final march, a 13-play, 81-yard drive, was a thing of beauty as Michael Robinson both passed and ran the squad down the field in 1:53. About the only thing Penn State did wrong that final drive, which was capped by Robinson's three-yard quarterback draw was leave just one second too many on the clock.

While the praises may ring hollow in the midst of a loss—stop the whining about the officials—remember a team that couldn't score more than four points against Iowa a year ago.

Maybe the biggest disappointment was a defense that has been so strong for so long. After cornerback Alan Zemaitis made a huge play by stripping the ball from Michigan quarterback Chad Henne and returning it 35 yards for a score, Penn State allowed two touchdown drives and a field goal in the final 11:39.

For a unit that was ranked 16th nationally in total defense coming into the game, the fourth quarter proved to be a nightmare. A look at a tired and limping Chris Harrell ambling up the players tunnel after the game could indicate that this group finally ran out of gas from the amount of playing time it has had to play this season.

It certainly wasn't helped by the Nittany Lions' kickoff coverage, which allowed Michigan returns to its 45 and 47 in its two fourth-quarter scoring drives. Someone besides Ethan Kilmer is going to have to make some tackles on this unit.

Henne's game-winner to Mario Manningham may have put a fork in the Nittany Lions this day, but it didn't end what still has a chance for big returns.

Think about it. Is there anyone left on Penn State's schedule that it won't be favored against?

OPPOSITE PAGE: **Wide receivers coach Mike McQueary stares in disbelief at the action on the field.** *Tom Pidgeon/Getty Images*

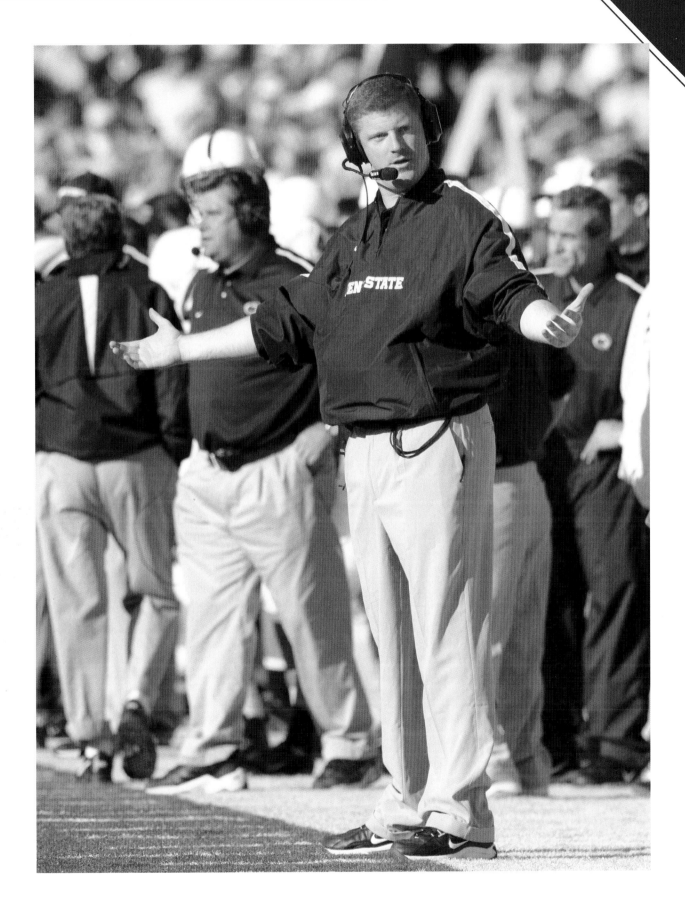

The Nittany Lions' next two opponents are Illinois (at Champaign) and Purdue (at home), both winless in the conference. Wisconsin, which has given up 129 points in four conference games, is next and the season concludes at Michigan State, which was bounced by Ohio State.

Given what most of Nittany Nation has seen over the past few seasons, this team fosters optimism.

One second won't change that.

"We've played two great football games, three really. These kids have hung in there. I'm proud of them. I don't know what else I could say. I'm proud of them; I'm disappointed for them."

— Joe Paterno,
Penn State coach

RIGHT: **Offensive tackle Levi Brown (67) watches grimly as a play unfolds.** *Tom Pidgeon/Getty Images*

POPPING CHAMPAIGN

BY JEFF RICE

His helmet had been long since packed away, his hands buried first in his blue quarterback's muff and then the pockets of a blue parka. The week before, Michael Robinson had done some great work late and then stood on the sideline watching helplessly as Chad Henne and Michigan came back to beat his Nittany Lions on the final play.

This day, Penn State's senior quarterback did some quick and efficient work early, then stood on the sideline and watched Illinois helplessly attack a deficit from which there was no coming back.

Robinson completed 11-of-18 passes for 194 yards and four touchdowns, and ran seven times for 69 yards and two more scores as the No. 12 Nittany Lions put Ann Arbor well behind them with a 63-10 domination of Illinois at Memorial Stadium.

"He gets better all the time," Penn State head coach Joe Paterno said of Robinson, echoing his statements from the week before. "If somebody's better than he is, he's gotta be awfully good."

RIGHT: Penn State quarterback Michael Robinson rushes for a touchdown to put the Nittany Lions up 49-3 in the second quarter. Robinson scored twice and connected with receivers for an additional four touchdowns against the Illini.
Raul Vasquez/Belleville News-Democrat

Penn State (7-1, 4-1 Big Ten) allowed a field goal on the game's first possession before reeling off 63 unanswered points. Illinois (2-5, 0-4) finally answered with a two-yard touchdown pass from backup quarterback Chris Pazan to backup tailback Rashard Mendenhall with 2:19 to play.

Paterno, who was surprised to know that he picked up his 350th career win, said he wasn't concerned about a letdown after a crushing 27-25 loss to Michigan the week before but was afraid his team would get tired working itself out in practices during the week.

The Nittany Lions showed evidence of neither.

With star receiver Derrick Williams back in State College with a broken arm, Robinson and Penn State's remaining receivers put on a dazzling first-quarter aerial display.

Deon Butler caught two touchdown passes, set the school single-season record for touchdown catches by a freshman (six) and led all receivers with four catches for 95 yards, all in the first half.

Senior wideout Ethan Kilmer opened Penn State's scoring with a 35-yard touchdown reception and five other Nittany Lions caught at least one pass before Paterno pulled the plug on the passing game early in the second half.

"My job was easy," Robinson said. "All I had to do was get it to them."

Most of the starters on Penn State's defense joined Robinson on the sideline in a well-deserved second-half rest, ignoring the late-evening chill and cheering on the second-stringers, many of whom hadn't played in at least a month.

Backup quarterback Anthony Morelli entered the game during Penn State's final drive of the second quarter. Third-stringer Paul Cianciolo lined up under center early in the fourth quarter. Tailbacks Rodney Kinlaw and Austin Scott both got more carries than first-stringer Tony Hunt.

OPPOSITE PAGE: **Tailback Austin Scott eludes Illinois' Charles Bailey in the second quarter. Scott carried the ball 14 times for 57 yards.**

Raul Vasquez/Belleville News-Democrat

	1st	2nd	3rd	4th	Final
Penn State	28	28	7	0	63
Illinois	3	0	0	7	10

Scoring Summary

ILL—Reda 41-yard field goal, 12 plays, 57 yards in 4:46
PSU—Kilmer 35-yard pass from Robinson (Kelly kick), three plays, 67 yards in 1:16
PSU—Butler 31-yard pass from Robinson (Kelly kick), six plays, 65 yards in 1:13
PSU—Butler 19-yard pass from Robinson (Kelly kick), nine plays, 52 yards in 2:20
PSU—Hall 3-yard pass from Robinson (Kelly kick), three plays, 38 yards in 0:36
PSU—Connor 18-yard fumble recovery (Kelly kick)
PSU—Robinson 4-yard run (Kelly kick), eight plays, 57 yards in 3:10
PSU—Robinson 31-yard run (Kelly kick), five plays, 60 yards in 1:47
PSU—Kinlaw 1-yard run (Kelly kick), four plays, 28 yards in 0:58
PSU—McCready 76-yard interception return (Kelly kick)
ILL—Mendenhall 2-yard pass from Pazan (Reda kick), 12 plays, 91 yards in 4:20

Team Statistics

Category	PSU	ILL
First Downs	19	15
Rushes-Yards (Net)	46-221	37-111
Passing Yards (Net)	217	133
Passes Att-Comp-Int	20-12-0	31-18-2
Total Offense Plays-Yards	66-438	68-244
Punt Returns-Yards	9-148	2-18
Kickoff Returns-Yards	2-109	8-132
Punts (Number-Avg)	5-43.4	9-50.2
Fumbles-Lost	1-0	1-1
Penalties-Yards	4-35	10-83
Possession Time	29:48	30:12
Sacks By (Number-Yards)	4-20	0-0

Individual Statistics

Rushing: Penn State-Robinson 7-69; Scott 14-57; King 2-37; Hunt 6-37; Kinlaw 10-14; Snow 2-10; Lawlor 1-4; Hahn 1-(-3); Team 3-(-4). **Illinois**-Thomas 9-45; Mendenhall 9-34; Halsey 5-27; Davis 1-3; Pazan 1-3; Brasic 11-0; McPhearson 1-(-1).

Passing: Penn State-Robinson 11-18-0-194; Morelli 1-2-0-23. **Illinois**-Brasic 8-16-0-49; Pazan 10-15-2-84.

Receiving: Penn State-Butler 4-95; Kilmer 2-44; Scott 2-23; Sargeant 1-23; Smolko 1-21; King 1-8; Hall 1-3. **Illinois**-Mendenhall 4-30; Warren 3-28; Jones 3-26; Hudson 2-16; Halsey 2-10; Davis 1-9; McPhearson 1-7; Thomas 1-4; McClendon 1-3.

Interceptions: Penn State-McCready 1-76; Scirrotto 1-0. **Illinois**-None.

Sacks (Unassisted-Assisted): Penn State-Rice 0-2; Paxson 0-1; Shipley 1-0; T. Shaw 0-1; Hali 1-0. **Illinois**-None.

Tackles (Unassisted-Assisted): Penn State-Connor 3-6; T. Shaw 2-5; Posluszny 2-4; Lowry 4-1; Ridenhour 1-4; Hali 1-4; Lee 1-3; Rice 1-3; Zemaitis 0-4; Fentress 3-0; J. Cianciolo 2-1; Gaines 1-2; Paxson 1-2; Shipley 1-2; Brown 1-2; McCready 0-3; Davis 2-0; Johnson 1-1. **Illinois**-Harrison 7-4; Leman 2-5; Mitchell 5-1; Ball 4-2; Willis 5-0; Walker 3-1; Knezetic 2-1; Kleckner 2-1; Moss 2-1; Miller 1-2; Weil 1-1; Bailey 1-1; Williams 1-1; Pittman 0-2; Matha 0-2.

ABOVE: **Deon Butler leaps in front of Illinois' Kevin Mitchell for a completion from Michael Robinson. Robinson and Butler connected twice for touchdowns in the first quarter.** *Raul Vasquez/Belleville News-Democrat*
OPPOSITE PAGE: **Illini tight end Melvin Bryant misses a pass thanks to heavy coverage by Penn State linebacker Sean Lee.** *Raul Vasquez/Belleville News-Democrat*

More than half of the announced crowd of 52,633 didn't see the need to hang around long enough to see those substitutions or to watch Illinois suffer its fourth loss of 20 points or more this season. The Illini managed just 244 total yards on 68 plays, turned the ball over three times and let Penn State do pretty much whatever it wanted.

The best player on the field for Illinois was punter Steve Weatherford, who averaged 50.2 yards

on his nine kicks. Starting quarterback Tim Brasic (8 of 16, 49 yards) was pulled for Chris Pazan, who threw for just 84 yards and a pair of second-half interceptions. With blitzes or three-man rushes, Penn State pressured Illinois quarterbacks all evening.

"I hope it sent a message out to the country," said defensive end Tamba Hali, who had one of four Penn State sacks. "Last week was a tough game, but we're a better team each week, and hopefully we were able to show it today."

Penn State's offense certainly sent a message. The Nittany Lions, who had been averaging 414 yards of offense per game, had 378 in the first half alone, wasting little time getting things going after a confidence-building opening drive by the Illini.

The Illini chose to receive the opening kickoff and looked smooth and competent on their opening possession. A holding penalty helped stall a 12-play, 57-yard drive at the Penn State 24, but a 41-yard Jason Reda field goal gave Illinois a 3-0 lead.

"It was a fast pace," Paterno said of the opening drive. "We weren't quite ready [defensively] for that faster pace."

That's where the Illini's highlight reel came to an abrupt end.

It took the Nittany Lions all of three plays and one minute, 16 seconds to answer. Robinson found Kilmer on a short crossing pattern, and the special teams star out-raced Alan Ball and cruised up the sideline to the end zone.

Penn State's next possession, Robinson found Butler all alone behind a broken defense for a 31-yard touchdown connection; Butler added a 19-yard touchdown catch on the possession after that. By the time backup tight end Patrick Hall clutched his second touchdown reception of the season, a three-yarder from Robinson that made it 28-3 with 36 seconds remaining in the first quarter.

The Illini managed one more first-half first down after the four they picked up on the game's opening drive, while Penn State went on to set a school record for points in a half with 56.

Penn State's defense contributed to the explosion of points. Sophomore linebacker Dan Connor ran back a fumble 18 yards for a touchdown in the second quarter after Tim Shaw's hit on Brasic knocked it loose, while backup safety Nolan McCready ran a third-quarter interception of Pazan back 76 yards for a touchdown.

The Nittany Lions return home to face Purdue, winless in the Big Ten, on October 29. They had expected to play well, to wash the bitter taste of the week before out of their mouths, but they didn't dare dream of a performance such as this.

"It's the Big Ten, anything can happen," Robinson said. "But we felt like we could go out there and do some things. I didn't expect not to play the second half, but it happened that way."

27 CHRIS HARRELL

BIRTHDATE: 01/29/83 **BIRTHPLACE:** CLEVELAND, OH **HIGH SCHOOL:** EUCLID (EUCLID, OH)
MAJOR: ECONOMICS **POSITION:** SAFETY **HEIGHT:** 6'2" **WEIGHT:** 210 LBS

It is one of the sweet ironies of this season that Chris Harrell has emerged as one of Penn State's leading tacklers from his free safety spot.

Once maligned as an inept tackler, he is now one of the big hitters in a secondary that forms a Siegfried Line behind the front seven.

But once, three seasons and a neck injury ago, Harrell was drawn and quartered after missing two tackles against Iowa in a game that the Hawkeyes won 42-35 in overtime in Beaver Stadium.

Both misses occurred along the sideline. One resulted in a Hawkeyes touchdown, the other in a long gain. And after the game, on a radio talk show a caller blistered the then sophomore from Euclid, Ohio, barking, "That guy can't tackle," and demanding that he be benched forever.

No thought was given to the fact that Harrell was an emergency replacement for Calvin Lowry and Yaacov Yisrael at strong safety.

"That was probably the lowest point in my career here," said Harrell, who is second on the team in tackles with 57 behind linebacker Paul Posluszny (82). "But it ended up being a turning point. Because I realized how important I was to the team and I had a big part in what happened on the field.

"It was tough but I had help from a lot of the seniors on the defense. I was down on myself but they picked me up, kept showing they believed in what I could do on the field. But after the game, when I looked at the film, I saw I was in a position to make the play and all I had to do was what I had been taught."

Time and circumstances have proven Harrell's confidence to be well founded, to the point where in some defensive sets he is all alone on his side of the field.

"With the scheme we're running, adding [Justin] King at the nickel back, we have a lot of speed guys in there and teams try to run away from them. That puts me in a position to make plays.

"It's a huge turnaround. Now, they depend on me, give me the freedom to make plays. I enjoy it—the pressure. Earlier, I would have been nervous but after last season, being able to come back, I just enjoy being out there because it was almost taken away from me."

It was a routine play in a routine spring practice drill in 2004. A wide receiver ran a slant route, Harrell came up and blasted him. But on the way back to the defensive huddle he felt a mild pain in his neck but continued to practice.

The next morning in the weight room he tried to do a neck exercise and found he could not move his neck. The Penn State medical staff ordered MRIs and X-rays, ran a number of tests and found an old bone chip in his neck as well as a hairline fracture of one of the vertebrae. Copies of the tests were sent to various doctors around the country, soliciting their opinions.

Meanwhile, Harrell was in limbo, waiting for a decision to be made.

"Initially, our trainers were not sure if anyone could play with that injury," he said. "One doctor said that the break was something that wouldn't catch much impact and if I waited out one season and did the rehab, I should be all right."

But no one was willing to make a definitive statement, especially with the injury to Adam Taliaferro so fresh in everyone's mind. So Harrell waited.

"I tried to be prepared if I had to finish school and go out into the regular work force," said Harrell, who is scheduled to graduate in December. "At that time I was really happy with my choice of a major because I was hearing good things about how I'd have no problem finding a job. Everything sounded good but I wanted to be out there playing football."

Instead he played the waiting game. Finally, Dr. Wayne Sebastianelli, director of athletic medicine at Penn State, cleared Harrell to resume playing. But as a precautionary measure, it was decided that Harrell should sit out last season to give the injury time to heal and for him to go through a full regimen of rehabilitation. This past spring he was back in pads. But even then, there was one more hurdle to clear.

"In practice I had a big collision and coach [Brian] Norwood and I looked at each other," he recalled. "I had no pain. I knew then I could put it all behind me."

What no one could have known then, and only a few believed possible, was that this team would be vying for a Big Ten title. From 4-7 to 6-1 is a Hollywood turnaround.

And it really began to gain momentum in the Northwestern game. That was exactly the kind of game they've lost the past two seasons.

"On that last drive, when we started losing yards, some people on the sidelines were thinking, 'Here we go again.' Before we couldn't make the big play, didn't have players to make it," Harrell said. "But as soon as [Smolko] caught that ball we knew we were going to get into position to at least make a field goal."

In truth, the majority of the players on this team believe that the road to recovery began with the fourth-quarter goal line stand that saved a win over Indiana last November. That carried over to a win over Michigan State in the season finale and now the Nittany Lions just had an eight-game winning streak ended by Michigan 27-25.

"In the spring, we were all saying that we were 2-0, not 0-0," said Harrell. "The momentum started with that goal line stand. Now, we just want to keep winning, keep playing our style of game."

And that is?

"Playing really, really aggressive defense," is how Harrell described it. "Offensively, we pound the ball inside then try to make big plays using our speed on the outside."

That speed came in with freshmen Derrick Williams, Justin King, Deon Butler and Jordan Norwood. Harrell saw their potential immediately.

"You always hear about young players coming in and how good they are," he said. "But sometimes you doubt it, you think, 'I've been here this long and I'm still developing,' but the first time they caught a pass I could see they were ready to play. And they have the advantage of going against a very experienced secondary every day in practice. They get to see what the best looks like and that has to help them."

In turn, they have helped all of the long-suffering upperclassmen turn around a program that was sliding deeper into mediocrity with every loss. Now there is a confidence in the huddle that was missing the past two years.

"Our goal now is to win every game," Harrell said. "We've come from so far down. We've been through the ups and downs. No we want to be at the top where Penn State belongs."

By Ron Bracken

Nabil K. Mark/Centre Daily Times

PSU STILL ON TRACK

BY JEFF RICE

B undled in blue and white, the third-largest crowd in Beaver Stadium history made its way through the exits, trying to figure out how to digest its team's latest win.

"We are!" came a faint cheer. The scattered response in unison: "Penn State!" was even fainter.

On a brisk homecoming afternoon, the Nittany Lions delivered another win, their eighth of the season, over a desperate and dangerous Purdue team. Penn State's 33-15 triumph before 109,476 was more sloppy than satisfying, more grit than glitz.

But, as quarterback Michael Robinson put it, "We got a 'W.' I'm happy."

Behind a big day from junior tailback Tony Hunt, a tough performance from its defense and with just enough big plays to keep the Boilermakers at bay, No. 11 Penn State (8-1, 5-1 Big Ten) stayed tied with No. 15 Wisconsin atop the conference standings. The Nittany Lions will meet the Badgers at 3:30 p.m. on November 5 in Beaver Stadium.

Hunt led all rushers with 129 yards on 24 carries, and Robinson added 96 more on 19 carries as the Nittany Lions, who were held to 18 rushing yards on 17 carries by Purdue last season, tallied 303 yards rushing on 55 carries. However, some uncharacteristic red-zone struggles and a pair of Penn State turnovers kept the struggling

Boilermakers (2-6, 0-5) in the game until the fourth quarter.

"We let them hang around and hang around and hang around," said Penn State coach Joe Paterno. "I thought, 'Yeah, we're gonna blow this one.'"

Behind senior quarterback Brandon Kirsch, who relieved ineffective sophomore Curtis Painter in the second half, Purdue cut Penn State's lead to 23-15 with 9:50 left in the game on a four-yard touchdown run by Kirsch and a two-point conversion.

Hunt and Robinson then went to work as Penn State drove 61 yards in eight plays—all rushes—to set up Kevin Kelly's fourth field goal of the day, a 22-yarder that put the Nittany Lions up 26-15.

Calvin Lowry intercepted Kirsch on Purdue's next play from scrimmage, and a brisk seven-play, 53-yard drive capped by BranDon Snow's four-yard touchdown run, his second of the day, finally put the Boilermakers away.

"A couple mistakes, a couple penalties against them hurt them, but they have talent," said Penn

OPPOSITE PAGE: **Penn State fullback BranDon Snow dives across the goal line for a touchdown at the end of the game. Snow rushed for two touchdowns against Purdue.** *Nabil K. Mark/Centre Daily Times*

State outside linebacker Dan Connor, who had seven tackles. "They hung around, and we had to keep pressing; we couldn't let down. We had to keep pressing and keep playing basically until the end."

The Nittany Lions held the Boilermakers to just 277 yards of offense but led just 16-7 at the half. Two of Penn State's first three trips inside the 15-yard line yielded only field goals. On their third, the Nittany Lions needed six plays and two Boilermaker penalties from the Purdue two-yard line to finally crack the end zone, which they did on a one-yard touchdown run from Robinson with just more than eight minutes remaining in the second quarter.

"I think we got too cute," said Paterno of his offense, which had scored 21 touchdowns in 34 red-zone visits (62 percent) prior to this game. "I think we got a little careless, plus the fact that they're a good defensive team down there."

Purdue's defense, ranked last in the nation against the pass coming in, fought hard. It didn't get much help, once again, from its offense. Six-foot-nine wideout Kyle Ingraham was a handful, leading all receivers with seven catches for 77 yards, but Kirsch and Painter combined for 162 yards on 38 pass attempts and tailbacks Jerod Void and Kory Sheetz were held to 68 yards on 16 carries.

"We were able to move the ball, but they kind of get a little bit stingy toward the goal line, and it's hard on you," said Kirsch, a Lebanon native. "We came up a couple times with a couple crucial third downs that we didn't convert on, so I think if we converted those, the defense would have stayed off the field and we would have had some points on the board."

It was also a frustrating afternoon for Robinson, who completed just 13 of his 29 passes for 213 yards, no touchdowns and no interceptions and, though he was sacked just once, took several hard shots from a blitz-happy Purdue defense.

	1st	2nd	3rd	4th	Final
Purdue	7	0	0	8	15
Penn State	3	13	7	10	33

Scoring Summary
PSU—Kelly 27-yard field goal, 13 plays, 85 yards in 5:16
PUR—Painter 24-yard run (Jones kick), one play, 24 yards in 0:08
PSU—Kelly 25-yard field goal, seven plays, 31 yards in 2:31
PSU—Robinson 1-yard run (Kelly kick), eight plays, 80 yards in 3:53
PSU—Kelly 33-yard field goal, five plays, 60 yards in 0:34
PSU—Snow 2-yard run (Kelly kick), four plays, 42 yards in 2:08
PUR—Kirsch 4-yard run (Bryant rush), seven plays, 58 yards in 1:30
PSU—Kelly 22-yard field goal, eight plays, 61 yards in 4:09
PSU—Snow 4-yard run (Kelly kick), seven plays, 53 yards in 3:52

Team Statistics
Category	PUR	PSU
First Downs	14	29
Rushes-Yards (Net)	26-115	55-303
Passing Yards (Net)	162	213
Passes Att-Comp-Int	38-17-1	29-13-0
Total Offense Plays-Yards	64-277	84-516
Punt Returns-Yards	4-22	5-15
Kickoff Returns-Yards	4-63	2-67
Punts (Number-Avg)	11-40.2	7-42.4
Fumbles-Lost	1-1	2-2
Penalties-Yards	8-51	4-30
Possession Time	22:55	37:05
Sacks By (Number-Yards)	1-8	0-0

Individual Statistics
Rushing: Purdue-Void 10-57; Painter 4-29; Sheets 6-11; Kirsch 4-9; Jones 2-9.
Penn State-Hunt 24-129; Robinson 19-96; King 4-56; Norwood 1-17; Snow 2-6; Scott 2-5; Team 1-(-2); Golden 1-(-2); Kinlaw 1-(-2).

Passing: Purdue-Kirsch 11-21-1-102; Painter 6-17-0-60.
Penn State-Robinson 13-29-0-213.

Receiving: Purdue-Ingraham 7-77; Sheets 4-26; Bryant 2-29; Hare 2-16; Davis 1-10; Void 1-4.
Penn State-Norwood 4-59; Hunt 4-57; Butler 2-51; Golden 2-25; Smolko 1-21.

Interceptions: Purdue-None.
Penn State-Lowry 1-0.

Sacks (Unassisted-Assisted): Purdue-Bick 1-0.
Penn State-None.

Tackles (Unassisted-Assisted): Purdue-Pollard 5-6; Hall 4-7; Bick 7-2; Ninkovich 5-3; Logan 5-1; R. Williams 4-1; Villarreal 2-3; Edwards 3-1; Iwuchukwu 3-1; Smith 3-1; Spencer 2-1; Avril 1-2; Whittington 2-0.
Penn State-Harrell 6-4; Connor 3-4; Kilmer 5-1; Posluszny 4-2; Rice 0-5; Zemaitis 3-1; Alford 2-2; Lowry 2-2; Phillips 3-0; T. Shaw 2-1; Hali 1-2.

OPPOSITE PAGE: **In spite of Boilermaker Zach Logan's defense, wideout Deon Butler gathers in a long pass during the first half.** *Nabil K. Mark/Centre Daily Times*

ABOVE: Penn State holder Jason Ganter (9) celebrates a Kevin Kelly (23) field goal against Purdue in the second quarter. Kelly kicked four field goals during the game. *Craig Houtz/Centre Daily Times*
OPPOSITE PAGE: Safety Calvin Lowry (10), Paul Posluszny (31) and Deon Butler (3) celebrate Lowry's fourth-quarter interception. *Nabil K. Mark/Centre Daily Times*

Robinson did lose a second-quarter fumble, which led to a few tense minutes involving the officials, the crowd and Paterno.

Purdue's Brandon Villarreal recovered an apparent Robinson fumble at his own 45-yard line. But the officials ruled the ball was down, and Penn State's punt team took the field. Then things got hazy. The Purdue defense took its time getting lined up, sending the crowd and Paterno into a fury. The officials then stopped the game to allow the replay official to review the ruling, and it was overturned, giving the Boilermakers the football.

Penn State's defense, however, was right there to force a three-and-out. The Nittany Lions weren't as fortunate on their first turnover, a fumbled punt by Calvin Lowry that the Boilermakers' Void recovered at the Penn State 24-yard line. Painter found a gaping lane on an option the very next play and raced untouched into the end zone. It was the first time the Nittany Lions had trailed at home since the second quarter against Ohio State.

Penn State added to its lead with a quick five-play, 60-yard drive in the final 36 seconds of the first half. A 14-yard scamper by Hunt, a 20-yard catch by Jordan Norwood, and a 12-yard reception by Hunt moved Penn State to the Purdue 30, and a pass-interference call against Purdue got the Nittany Lions to the 14. A Robinson incompletion left one second left on the clock, just enough time for Kelly to nail a 33-yarder.

The Nittany Lions earned some breathing room early in the second half. Rodney Kinlaw's 58-yard kickoff return helped set up a two-yard plunge by Snow, his first career touchdown run and just his fourth career carry. An unlikely weapon in Penn State's multi-pronged attack, the senior fullback understood the importance of a win that, unlike many this season, didn't come easily.

"It's a credit to the team, a credit to the defense," he said. "The defense put up great numbers, had a great game."

Snow paused, before adding: "We made plays when it counted."

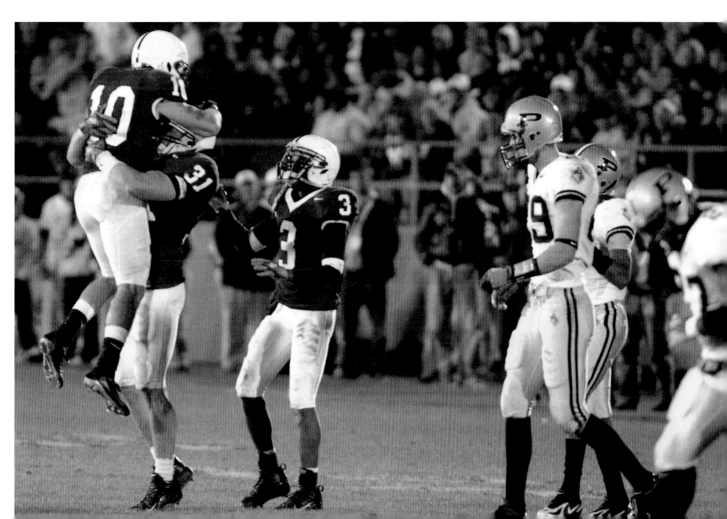

67 LEVI BROWN

BIRTHDATE: 03/16/84 BIRTHPLACE: JACKSONVILLE, NC HIGH SCHOOL: GRANBY HIGH SCHOOL (NORFOLK, VA)
MAJOR: LABOR & INDUSTRIAL RELATIONS POSITION: TACKLE HEIGHT: 6'5" WEIGHT: 324 LBS

It was a bad idea and Levi Brown wanted no part of it. Nope. No way. He was a defensive lineman when he arrived at Penn State and he was going to be one when he left. Period.

Today, when the Nittany Lions offense takes the field against Purdue, Brown will be lined up at left tackle—for the third year in a row. You can't miss him. He's the oak tree wearing No. 67.

So what happened? How did he come to this place he once loathed?

Let's go back to 2003.

Brown reluctantly accepted the switch to offense three years ago.

Brown had spent his freshman season as a redshirt defensive lineman just as he had envisioned he would when he left Granby (Virginia) High School.

But once he had spent a year at Penn State, playing on the scout team, going through spring drills, there were hints that his days in a four-point stance were numbered.

And they came not from the coaches but from his teammates.

"A lot of the offensive guys were talking to me, saying, 'You're coming to offense. It's just a matter of time.' They were waiting for me. They told me they had a seat waiting for me at the first [offensive line] meeting."

Brown didn't want to hear it, didn't want nothin' to do with no offensive line meeting. He was a defensive lineman from cleats to helmet.

Until one day just prior to the opening of preseason drills, he wound up in a conversation with a couple of coaches, who told him that they recognized he had great ability and that they would have to find a place for him on the team.

That was one conversation. The next one changed his career.

"I love defense," he said. "My hopes and dreams were to play defense. And the coaches said that's where they wanted me to play. But after I got here and they evaluated me, saw how I played defense, they told me I was better suited on offense so Joe [Paterno] decided to make the change. I believe in Joe and he believed in me.

"But at first I was a little shocked and a little hurt at the same time," he remembered. "They were telling me where I had to play and I had no choice. I was thinking, 'I don't want to do this. Who do you think you are, telling me where I have to play?' I did a lot of second-guessing, didn't want to do the things they wanted me to do. I was trying to get them to put me back on defense. I'd always be looking over at the defensive field to see what was going on over there."

He had gone from a field of dreams to a field of screams. In 2003, the Nittany Lions fell to a 3-9 record, the worst of Paterno's career. And the offensive line was a focal point for the critics.

"When things go wrong the finger gets pointed at someone," said Brown, who stepped in and started all 12 games at left tackle.

The situation barely improved last fall when a 4-9 record was the best the Nittany Lions could do as they scored a total of 21 points in four Big Ten losses.

This year, they're one second away from being unbeaten through eight games. The offense has exploded with Michael Robinson at the controls and a fleet of freshman wide receivers stretching defenses.

And up front it's the same guys who were blistered for their ineptitude a year ago. What happened?

"We all stuck together," said the six-foot-five, 324-pound Brown. "We look at film together, see our mistakes and work at getting better.

"We just got tired of losing. They say you play like you practice and we have not had a bad week of practice yet. Everyone wants to get to one of those BCS bowls."

If they win out, they will. If it hadn't been for the Chad Henne-to-Mario Manningham pass, there would be little doubt. That loss will take a while to get over.

"I don't think we've got all of the stuff from the Michigan game out of our system yet," Brown said. "We have three more games to get that all out of our system. But the Illinois game was a start.

"We all signed up to come here to have a season like this."

There was a time when Brown, who will graduate in December, couldn't have pictured himself being in this position. He was a late-comer to the game.

"I didn't start playing until I was in ninth grade," he explained. "I was way too heavy to play [in the youth leagues]. I played baseball. I wanted to go play in the major leagues. But two of my friends kept calling me a punk because I didn't play football. One day, I was walking across the JV football field on my way to baseball practice and I decided to try it.

"I didn't really know what was going on at first but I picked it up pretty quick. But when I first started it wasn't me knocking people on their butt. They called some guys up from the JVs to work with the varsity and I was lucky enough to be one of them. But those varsity guys just killed me. Practice after practice they were knocking me all over the place. It was an interesting experience."

Once Brown made the transition and began to flourish, his dreams switched from baseball to football. And not just on Saturdays.

"If you're playing football and [the NFL is] not your dream, that's a problem," he said. "It's mandatory to have that goal, to play on Saturdays and then on Sundays. It has to happen. It is your job to get there."

That's long term. In the short term, his job and the job of all of his teammates, is to win as many games as possible, to live the dream they all had when they were coming out of high school.

"We had two horrible seasons where things didn't go our way," he said. "We just want to be able to have success, to experience some of the things everyone thought we'd have when we came here. And we've been in high-profile games, been on national TV and been able to go out and have fun. This year, even when we make mistakes we don't get down on ourselves. To have a season like this, when the chips are falling our way, we're so grateful. I cherish every moment of it."

But what if, one day before practice, Paterno approached him and said he'd give him the opportunity to go back to his roots, to get down in that four-point stance again and just blow past a blocker into the backfield?

"Right now I'd have to turn it down," he said. "If it was just for one play in a game, I might take that, just to have fun. I might not love offense but I like it."

By Ron Bracken

Craig Houtz/Centre Daily Times

ROAR TO THE FORE

BY JEFF RICE

In and out of the spotlight, on and off the stat sheet, at the beginning, middle and end of the biggest game of their careers, Penn State's seniors made their presence felt.

They made a game that might have decided the Big Ten championship seem like a scrimmage for the first three quarters.

And they made another step—perhaps the biggest yet—toward cementing their place in Nittany Lion history.

Jumping out to a quick 21-0 lead and answering late Wisconsin rallies with quick strikes of their own, those seniors carried No. 10 Penn State (9-1, 6-1 Big Ten) to a 35-14 defeat of the No. 14 Badgers (8-2, 5-2) before 109,865, the second-largest crowd in Beaver Stadium history.

Twenty-five seniors ran out of the south end zone tunnel one last time. Thirteen of them started, and their prints were all over this win. Defensive end Tamba Hali had four sacks and set a school record with seven tackles for loss. Quarterback Michael Robinson ran for 125 yards and threw for two touchdowns. And Penn State's senior-

RIGHT: Senior defensive end Tamba Hali sacks Wisconsin's quarterback John Stocco in the first half. Stocco was sacked nine times, twice by Hali.

Nabil K. Mark/Centre Daily Times

ABOVE: **Freshman wide receiver Jordan Norwood tries to shake off Wisconsin's Roderick Rogers after making a catch.** *Nabil K. Mark/Centre Daily Times*

dominated defense held vaunted Wisconsin tailback Brian Calhoun to just 38 yards on 20 carries.

The Nittany Lions completed just their third perfect home season in 13 years in the Big Ten and took over sole possession of first place in the conference with one game remaining. Penn State is idle next week and then travels to East Lansing to face Michigan State on November 19.

"They've been a great bunch of kids who have stuck together, who have stayed with the staff," said

Penn State coach Joe Paterno of his seniors. "We talked a lot and said they had the makings of a good football team if they would just stick with it. And when they do it and they have success, you can't help but feel really good about it."

There was little else but good feeling during the first half, when the Nittany Lions scored touchdowns on three of their first four possessions. Penn State's offense fell asleep during the third quarter, however, and the Badgers closed to within two scores early in the fourth when Calhoun scored on a one-yard touchdown run with 12:27 to play.

"We started off pretty hot," said freshman wide receiver Deon Butler, who finished with five catches for 125 yards and two touchdowns. "We got out there, got 21 [points], but then we staggered a little bit."

It was a senior who answered with a big play—a senior who has done a lot of answering this season. Robinson, who had been having trouble connecting with his receivers after a terrific start, found a streaking Butler in traffic for a 47-yard touchdown pass.

"The thing about Michael Robinson is he's played so well in the clutch when he's had to make plays," Paterno said.

That score proved huge when Wisconsin tallied another touchdown two possessions later. A 65-yard strike from Stocco (19 of 34, 313 yards, two interceptions, one touchdown) to Jonathan Orr set up Stocco's 18-yard touchdown pass to Brandon White.

Still, Penn State wasn't done. A late five-play, 46-yard drive—41 of those yards from junior tailback Tony Hunt—and a 10-yard touchdown run from Hunt sent the seniors off in style.

"There were some times where it looked like momentum might have been swinging their way," said center E.Z. Smith, one of four senior starters on the offensive line, "and then right when it happened we were able to put a score back on the board."

The offensive line carried the offense to more than 500 yards for the fourth time this season. The defense, shoved around by the Badgers during a 16-3 loss in Madison last year, held Wisconsin to minus-11 yards rushing and sacked Stocco nine times. The special teams kept the Badgers firmly pinned on their side of the field.

"We were beaten by a very good football team today," said Wisconsin coach Barry Alvarez, who lost in Beaver Stadium for just the second time in five visits. "They are very solid on both sides of the ball. They create a lot of problems for you, especially offensively."

	1st	2nd	3rd	4th	Final
Wisconsin	0	0	0	14	14
Penn State	7	14	0	14	35

Scoring Summary

PSU—Butler 43-yard pass from Robinson (Kelly kick), five plays, 78 yards in 1:38

PSU—Hunt 9-yard run (Kelly kick), 11 plays, 81 yards in 4:00

PSU—Snow 3-yard run (Kelly kick), seven plays, 80 yards in 2:29

WIS—Calhoun 1-yard run (Mehlhaff kick), seven plays, 89 yards in 3:01

PSU—Butler 47-yard pass from Robinson (Kelly kick), five plays, 69 yards in 2:03

WIS—White 18-yard pass from Stocco (Mehlhaff kick), four plays, 81 yards in 0:57

PSU—Hunt 10-yard run (Kelly kick), five plays, 46 yards in 2:25

Team Statistics

Category	WIS	PSU
First Downs	18	24
Rushes-Yards (Net)	34-(-11)	47-282
Passing Yards (Net)	313	238
Passes Att-Comp-Int	34-19-2	28-13-2
Total Offense Plays-Yards	68-302	75-520
Punt Returns-Yards	1-8	4-55
Kickoff Returns-Yards	6-127	2-28
Punts (Number-Avg)	7-42.6	4-39.8
Fumbles-Lost	0-0	0-0
Penalties-Yards	4-35	5-53
Possession Time	28:21	31:39
Sacks By (Number-Yards)	1-7	9-64

Individual Statistics

Rushing: **Wisconsin**-Calhoun 20-38; Stanley 1-2; Stocco 13-(-51).
Penn State-Hunt 24-151; Robinson 16-125; King 3-6; Snow 2-4; Team 2-(-4).

Passing: **Wisconsin**-Stocco 19-34-2-313.
Penn State-Robinson 13-28-2-238.

Receiving: **Wisconsin**-Calhoun 6-48; Williams 5-102; Orr 3-89; White 2-44; Daniels 2-26; Pociask 1-4.
Penn State-Butler 5-125; Golden 2-45; Hunt 2-35; Norwood 2-19; Kilmer 2-14.

Interceptions: **Wisconsin**-Hampton 1-22; Langford 1-25.
Penn State-Zemaitis 1-0; Lowry 1-0.

Sacks (Unassisted-Assisted): **Wisconsin**-Stocco 1-0.
Penn State-Hali 2-4; Posluszny 0-2; Rice 0-2; Alford 0-1; Shipley 1-0; T. Shaw 1-0; Connor 0-1.

Tackles (Unassisted-Assisted): **Wisconsin**-Stellmacher 5-7; Sanders 6-4; Zalewski 3-7; Rogers 6-1; Shaughnessy 4-1; Watkins 3-2; Monty 1-4; Hayden 3-0; Newkirk 3-0; Stocco 2-0; Crooks 1-1; Langford 0-2.
Penn State-Posluszny 5-7; Hali 3-6; Connor 3-5; T. Shaw 4-3; Harrell 4-2; Rice 1-5; Lowry 5-0; Phillips 3-0; Paxson 2-1; Kilmer 0-2.

ABOVE: **Tony Hunt breaks away for a long run. Hunt rushed for 151 yards and scored two touchdowns.**
Nabil K. Mark/Centre Daily Times

That Penn State offense struck quickly and decisively on its opening drive. Robinson found Terrell Golden on a tough 21-yard out pass and then hooked up with Butler, who beat Wisconsin cornerback Brett Bell deep for a 43-yard touchdown. Hunt, who ran for a career-high 151 yards, doubled the lead with a nine-yard touchdown run four seconds into the second quarter, and cornerback Alan Zemaitis, one quarter of Penn State's all-senior secondary, intercepted Stocco in the end zone on the following possession.

"I got a lot of pressure, but I think a lot of that is because we got away from what we wanted to do," Stocco said. "When you're in a situation where they know you're going to pass, they are going to get pressure on you."

Wisconsin had entered the game with a points-per-game average of 39.7, the school's highest in the modern era. Calhoun had been averaging 135 rushing yards per game, second-highest in the Big Ten, but never got it going against a swarming Penn State defense. None of his runs was longer than eight yards.

"All this talk all week about Calhoun this, Calhoun that," Hunt said, "that really motivates our defense."

Apparently, it motivated Hunt as well. The junior tailback racked up 111 of his yards in the second half, when Paterno, as he has often done this season when the Nittany Lions are protecting a lead, turned to the running game.

Junior Paul Posluszny led Penn State with 12 tackles, but the day belonged to the seniors. Paterno said he let Robinson, the first Nittany Lion off the bus, walk a little bit ahead of him. Lowry, the beleaguered punt returner, had a career-best return of 43 yards. Robinson set the school's single-season total offense record previously held by Kerry

ABOVE: **Deon Butler grabs a 43-yard touchdown pass from Michael Robinson in the first quarter. Butler scored again for the Nittany Lions in the fourth quarter.** *Nabil K. Mark/Centre Daily Times*

Collins, who quarterbacked Penn State to an undefeated season in 1994.

The comparisons to that season aren't ending there.

"Besides the '94 team, we want to be the only other team that has a Big Ten championship here," Smith said. "We want to be a team that's remembered in the history books."

20 TIM SHAW

BIRTHDATE: 03/27/84 BIRTHPLACE: EXETER, ENGLAND HIGH SCHOOL: CLARENCEVILLE (LIVONIA, MI)
MAJOR: MANAGEMENT POSITION: LINEBACKER HEIGHT: 6'1" WEIGHT: 233 LBS

This is the kind of game Tim Shaw has been waiting for, a bare-knuckle, mano-a-mano rock fight.

Put the skirts on the quarterbacks, the ballet slippers on the wideouts and send them to the sidelines. This one's for the big boys. There's going to be blood and spit and snot and bruises aplenty.

In other words, it's going to be the kind of game where Shaw's going to be needed in the middle instead of being yanked when the Nittany Lions go to their nickel package every third snap. He hates that.

"No one wants to be on the sidelines," he said in an even tone.

He goes there in part because he's a victim of his own versatility. He spent two years as part of an experiment where the coaches tried him on offense, then defense, and then both. He was a tailback, an H-back, an outside linebacker and an inside linebacker.

Even this fall he was outside because Dan Connor had gotten himself entangled in some legal issues. But once Connor was cleared to play, he went outside and Shaw was moved into the middle. And at the same time, he was being used at the H-back spot.

"When we'd go to the nickel drill in practice they'd pull me and send me to the offense," Shaw explained without rancor. "I didn't like that one bit. Now, every time we go to the nickel, I go to the sidelines.

"Since I've been at linebacker they've still played me on offense a few times. Moving around is not fun; no one will tell you that it is."

Connor's return and the evolution of the offense into a much more versatile and dangerous unit has allowed Shaw to stay on defense. But down-and-distance plus an opponent's tendencies dictates how much he's on the field.

Passing teams like Purdue rob Shaw of snaps. Wisconsin's a team that lines up five snow plows, tucks a 270-pound fullback behind them and a tailback behind all that muscle and then says, "Guess what we're gonna do?"

Shaw will be in the middle of that mass while Connor and Paul Posluszny are on the outside looking in.

"Inside every play you're smacking someone who weighs 300 pounds, or you're trying to get off them," Shaw said. "It's a completely different world in the middle. You use your speed to get to the outside to make a play or you're just trying to battle those big guys, trying to see over them to see where the ball's going.

"You have to be smart and use great technique—I'm still working on that. But the smarter you are the better position you'll be in to make the play. You have to know when to go smack the lineman or try to get around him."

The penalty for making a bad decision is usually painful.

"You get run over," Shaw said. "That happens more frequently than I'd like to see."

Sometimes it's because the linemen skirt the rules.

"OK, I'll say it, they don't call holding on every play, but they could," Shaw says with a wry smile. "The difference between a great offensive line and an average one is that they know how to hold. Coaches will look at film and ask my why I didn't make the tackle, why I couldn't get off this guy and it will be because he has me blocked, gripped. Those guys know all of the secrets and they know how to use their size against you."

Shaw has teamed with Posluszny and Connor to give the Nittany Lions their best linebacking trio since the 1999 group of LaVar Arrington, Brandon Short and Mac Morrison. And since they're all underclassmen, this unit could eventually rise to the level of the Shane Conlan-led 1986 group and might even approach the gold standard set by the 1968-69 group of Denny Onkotz, Jim Kates and Jack Ham. Time and productivity will determine that.

It's an interesting group. Posluszny and Connor were linebackers from the day they arrived at Penn State. Shaw, even though he played the position for four years in high school, was moved around and as a result, is playing catchup when it comes to the techniques and nuances of the position.

"I spent almost two years on the other side (offense) and that's big," he said. "Plus, I've played two positions, inside and outside. If something would happen to Dan I'd be back outside. Every day in practice I do both. I consider myself a pretty smart guy (he's got a 3.3 GPA in management) but it's tough getting where I want to get to. I guess it's a compliment to me that they think I can do that."

The three complement each other, which makes them such a solid unit. And yet they're all different.

"I wouldn't say we're great friends off the field because we're not," Shaw said matter-of-factly. "But we feel that together we can be great. We know we can become a great unit. We all have great gifts and athletic ability and we play well together. It's a great combination.

"One of the best things is when a team might get a long drive going against us and we can tell the big guys (defensive linemen) are getting tired and I'll look over at Paul and we both start smiling. We know we're in the best shape and we know we're the ones who have to pick it up. We know it's time to stop the drive, and he and I are the ones who are going to do it. We know we're not going to get tired. I don't get tired. Of course I'm not playing as much, but if I get tired everyone else out there is going to be dead."

Shaw is the oldest of the three, being a redshirt junior. Posluszny is a true junior and Connor is a true sophomore. They are different in other ways as well.

"Paul is perceived as the tough leader, a reliable guy, the guy everyone can count on to make a big play," is Shaw's assessment. "I see him as a great fundamental linebacker. He's instinctive.

"Dan is not so much instinctive, but he uses his athletic ability to make plays. He's a very smart player.

"I'm all over the place. I'm pretty smart but sometimes I count on my athletic ability too much. I'm not as far along as those two. Sometimes I run too fast and get out of position but that's because I'm anxious to make a play. I'm not as instinctive. Sometimes, I have to tell myself to just play but then I play too fast."

What he really wants to do is to make himself into the kind of linebacker who stays on the field, down-and-distance be damned.

"I've told Scrap (defensive coordinator Tom Bradley) that I'm going to learn that nickel position in the offseason, but right now I'll take what (playing time) I can get," he said. "I just want to be known as the dependable player, a leader, a hard worker, a tough guy you can count on. I want to be so good that I can't be taken out. I want to be the guy they need in there."

By Ron Bracken

ZEMAITIS KNEW THE DAY WOULD END LIKE THIS

BY RON BRACKEN

Alan Zemaitis could feel it coming, even in the small hours of Saturday morning.

He knew, just flat knew, that this was going to be one of those days.

He just didn't know it was going to be as good as it turned out for him and for his Penn State football team.

How could he? How could he have envisioned the Nittany Lions defense holding Wisconsin, a team some think invented the running game, to minus-11 yards on the ground? How could he have expected the Nittany Lions to sack John Stocco nine times or intercept him twice? How could he have forseen a 35-14 win over the 14th-ranked Badgers?

No, no one could have envisioned that without some chemical help.

All Zemaitis knew deep in his soul was that Saturday was going to be one of the best days in his life. Then he went out and lived it.

"Did you ever have a day when things seem perfect?" he said to a group of media clustered around an interview cubicle. "I woke up in the middle of the night, I was sprawled across the bed, the climate of the room was perfect and I knew I had a couple of more hours of sleep. Then I woke up, the sun was out and there was the smell of football in the air. People were firing up the grills."

Meanwhile, on the team buses headed for Beaver Stadium, the intensity was crackling.

"Everyone was real focused," added Zemaitis, who may be the most focused of all of the Nittany Lions, or at least the most intense. "If you've ever been around someone and even though they didn't say anything, you knew what they were thinking, that was it. It was like you could sense that if you just touched someone they would come at you.

"The buses pulled up and everyone was hitting the buses and that just got us wild. We were like caged animals."

At 3:30 p.m., their leashes were unsnapped and the beatings began. Wisconsin tailback Brian Calhoun had nowhere to run, Stocco had nowhere to hide as the Nittany Lions defense enveloped them like ground fog. It might have been this defense's finest hour. If not, it's on the short list.

"Today all we had to do was cover our man for a couple of seconds," Zemaitis added. "He (Stocco) didn't have time to get the ball out.

"I remember hearing people talking about other teams being tougher than us but on our defense there are some guys who are tougher than anyone I've known in my entire life. And when you put us all together, with all of the skills we possess, you're putting a masterpiece together."

The Badgers, who were tied with Penn State for the lead in the Big Ten going into the game, finally managed to get a drive together after falling behind 14-0 in the second quarter. They were perched on the Nittany Lion 5 when Stocco tried to hit tight end Owen Daniels in the back of the end zone. Zemaitis beat Daniels to the ball, and the Nittany Lions immediately drove 80 yards in seven plays to go up 21-0.

"I saw out of the corner of my eye that the tight end was off to my right," Zemaitis said. "I saw him sort of sit down in the back of the end zone. Someone else had jumped my guy and I saw the quarterback looking at the tight end and I just ran over there."

A 21-0 ditch was something the Badgers could not crawl out of on this day, even though they rallied for a pair of late touchdowns. But at no point did

ABOVE: **Penn State's Matt Rice (55) and Tamba Hali hug after the game against Wisconsin. The defense pummeled the Badgers all game.** *Nabil K. Mark/Centre Daily Times*

anyone get the sense that they were going to ruin Senior Day for Zemaitis and his classmates. This year is going way too well for them to allow that to happen in front of a crowd that has grown to love them.

"It's crazy," Zemaitis continued. "This year I finally began to understand what having a home-field advantage was all about. I never had that before, not even in high school. It's a feeling like this is our house and no one is going to come in here and push us around."

At least not this year. The past two years there was a different atmosphere, one that this bunch of seniors found galling. They were determined to purge it.

"We don't ever, ever, ever talk about the past," said Zemaitis, one of the defensive co-captains. "We don't talk about last week, three years ago, last year. With the senior leadership we have we have never taken our eyes off the prize."

And while head coach Joe Paterno said he will ease the practice schedule during the upcoming bye week, Zemaitis isn't expecting that to happen.

"No, we'll be banging," he said. "We'll have a game this week—we'll be playing each other. You guys just won't be invited."

Then it will be off to East Lansing, Michigan, for a season finale with a Michigan State team that is staggering toward the finish line. Penn State can clinch the Big Ten title outright if it beats the Spartans. Which is why Zemaitis was having nothing to do with celebrating the win over Wisconsin.

"We have so much more we can accomplish," Zemaitis said. "I was telling Anwar [Phillips] in the locker room that we just have to shower up, go home and get ready for another week."

Then he headed out into the November night, content with the ending to a perfect day.

LEFT: **Matt Rice, a senior, celebrates with the student section.** *Nabil K. Mark/Centre Daily Times*

PATERNO WORTHY OF COACH OF THE YEAR

BY RON BRACKEN

It's that time of year when the semifinalists and finalists for college football's numerous national awards are being announced.

If there's a position, right down to assistant manager in charge of shining shoes, there's an award for it. That's not necessarily a bad thing—managers are people, too. Undervalued, underesetimated, underappreciated people if you get right down to it. So maybe there should be a Kiwi Award. But that's a topic to be addressed at some future date.

What we're talking about here is the legitimate candidates for the Coach of the Year award. Who has done the best job guiding his team through the season, avoiding the upsets and pitfalls that are sprinkled across the autumn landscape?

The opinion that follows might surprise some of you, namely those who believe some sort of grudge exists between here and his office.

But if I had a vote to cast, it would be for Joe Paterno and the job he's done with the Penn State program this fall.

OK, you can wipe the look of disbelief off your face. It's true, and no, that choice is not the result of some mind-altering substance.

Credit goes where it's deserved, and Paterno deserves to be recognized for reversing the polarity of his program.

He said frequently during the course of this season that he never believed his program was that far away from returning to prominence but not many people believed him. Going into this season there were more unanswered questions about his team than there were on my algebra final.

Could Michael Robinson get the job done at quarterback? Who would catch the passes Robinson would throw? Could the offensive line keep the rush off Robinson? Who would take care of the place-kicking duties? Could the defensive line, minus Lavon Chisely and Ed Johnson, go the entire season without injuries sapping the depth?

Be honest with yourself. Would you have answered yes to all of those questions back in August?

Then there were the off-field incidents that further clouded the picture.

E.Z. Smith and Tyler Reed, two key returning veterans on the offensive line, had to work their way up from the basement of Paterno's doghouse to get back into the lineup.

Dan Connor got into a legal hassle that broke during preseason that kept him out of the lineup for the early part of the season, causing the defense to reshuffle the linebacking corps.

For a team that was struggling to shed the skin of a losing season, these were unwanted, potentially ruinous distractions.

But through it all Paterno kept the bus on the highway, maintaining his focus in a way only he can.

And here we are, in mid-November, with Penn State holding a 9-1 record, ranked sixth in the polls, in line for a conference title and a BCS bowl bid if it

OPPOSITE PAGE: **Penn State coach Joe Paterno always had faith that his teams were not far from success.**

Nabil K. Mark/Centre Daily Times

> *"I have never doubted this team . . . I never expected them to fold. I expected them to do just what they have done—to play just as hard as they could. I felt good about this team."*
>
> — Joe Paterno, Penn State coach

can take care of business in East Lansing on Saturday.

Yes, Charlie Weis has done a magnificent job at Notre Dame this fall. And in almost any other year, he would be a hands-down choice for every Coach of the Year Award. Who knows, he may win it this year, and if he does, who can say he's not deserving?

USC's Pete Carroll has operated under incredible pressure as the favorite to win a third straight national title. Mack Brown has lifted Texas to elite status, finally clearing that last hurdle of winning the big game by dispatching Ohio State in Columbus and beating Oklahoma. And Mike Shula has brought Alabama back to prominence, winning with a pedestrian offense.

Any ballot should have all of those names on it.

But the majority of the check marks should go in the block beside Paterno's name.

And they probably will because what he's done this fall is the national feel-good story. He's silenced the majority of his critics, at least for now, who were sure the game had passed him by.

Eventually, it will. No one beats the calendar in the Big Game. But he won this round when many thought he was headed for a TKO.

From somewhere deep in his being he summoned the energy and the will to win and infused it into his team. He has rewarded the true believers and convinced the majority of the doubters, at least to this point in this year.

In one man's poll, no one has done a better job this season.

OPPOSITE PAGE: **During previous seasons Paterno ardently defended Penn State's football legacy.**

Nabil K. Mark/Centre Daily Times

PENN STATE CAPTURES SHARE OF BIG TEN, BCS BID

BY JEFF RICE

J ust let things happen.

It's the simple yet powerful advice Michael Robinson offered to fellow tri-captains Alan Zemaitis and Paul Posluszny this preseason, when Joe Paterno assigned them the task of leading Penn State through what would become the greatest one-year turnaround in program history.

And it might be the best way to explain how the Nittany Lions did it.

Facing an erratic but talented Michigan State team in a state that has been all too unkind the past few years, No. 5 Penn State let things happen again, using big plays in every facet of the game to hold off the Spartans 31-22 before 75,005 in revamped Spartan Stadium and clinch a share of its second Big Ten championship and the conference's Bowl Championship Series bowl bid.

The Nittany Lions (10-1, 7-1 Big Ten) will play in the Orange, Fiesta or Rose bowl, depending on how the rest of the college football season shakes out.

Zemaitis recorded three of Penn State's four interceptions, Robinson ran for one touchdown and threw for another and the Nittany Lions' special

RIGHT: Penn State's Scott Paxson (41) bats an illegal forward pass back at Michigan State quarterback Drew Stanton (5) in the third quarter.
Craig Houtz/Centre Daily Times

teams came up the biggest when it mattered the most.

"We didn't play a real good football game," said a weary but happy Paterno, "but we made plays when we had to make them."

Penn State kept the Big Ten's most productive offense at bay early on but led just 3-0 with seven minutes to play in the second quarter. Then things started to happen.

Donnie Johnson blocked a Brandon Fields punt, and Matt Hahn recovered it in the end zone, extending the Nittany Lions' lead to 10-0. The Spartans went three plays and out, and then Robinson, who had overthrown receivers and watched them drop several of his passes early on, got the offense moving. He threw a screen pass to tailback Tony Hunt for 22 yards and then ran 33 yards into the end zone himself, making it 17-0 with 4:13 left before the half.

Spartans quarterback Drew Stanton completed 23-of-36 passes for 233 yards and led Michigan State (5-6, 2-6) to a pair of late touchdowns but threw a season-high four interceptions. The Spartans drove inside Penn State's 20-yard line five times but came away with just two scores.

"It goes back to the summer when we were training," said safety Calvin Lowry. "You put yourself in different scenarios in your head and how you're gonna finish."

Zemaitis picked off Stanton at his own one-yard line on Michigan State's first possession, and Johnson, who also blocked a punt against the Spartans last year, grabbed an interception in the end zone in the final seconds of the first half.

"It's just another case of me trying to do too much," said Stanton, who was Michigan State's leading rusher with 81 yards on 19 carries. "We were executing, doing a great job, and I was just trying to force too much."

	1st	2nd	3rd	4th	Final
Penn State	3	14	7	7	31
Michigan State	0	0	14	8	22

Scoring Summary
PSU—Kelly 32-yard field goal, 11 plays, 65 yards in 4:27
PSU—Hahn 0-yard blocked punt return (Kelly kick)
PSU—Robinson 33-yard run (Kelly kick), two plays, 55 yards in 0:28
MSU—Teague 25-yard run (Haughey kick), eight plays, 75 yards in 2:39
PSU—Butler 3-yard pass from Robinson (Kelly kick), three plays, four yards in 1:23
MSU—Scott 4-yard run (Haughey kick), 11 plays, 56 yards in 5:37
PSU—Hunt 1-yard run (Kelly kick), 10 plays, 64 yards in 4:27
MSU—Reed 15-yard pass from Stanton (Stanton rush), four plays, 27 yards in 1:15

Team Statistics
Category	PSU	MSU
First Downs	16	23
Rushes-Yards (Net)	39-188	42-168
Passing Yards (Net)	105	233
Passes Att-Comp-Int	20-10-0	36-23-4
Total Offense Plays-Yards	59-293	78-401
Punt Returns-Yards	1-19	3-15
Kickoff Returns-Yards	1-14	5-102
Punts (Number-Avg)	6-38.3	4-24.8
Fumbles-Lost	2-1	0-0
Penalties-Yards	4-24	7-55
Possession Time	26:20	33:40
Sacks By (Number-Yards)	2-21	0-0

Individual Statistics
Rushing: **Penn State**-Robinson 13-90; Hunt 20-89; Butler 1-6; Snow 2-4; Kinlaw 1-3; Team 2-(-4). **Michigan State**-Stanton 19-81; Teague 9-59; Caulcrick 9-28; Ringer 3-6; Scott, 1-4; Team 1-(-10).

Passing: **Penn State**-Robinson 10-20-0-105. **Michigan State**-Stanton 23-36-4-233.

Receiving: **Penn State**-Butler 4-46; Hunt 2-29; Smolko 2-7; Kilmer 1-12; Norwood 1-11. **Michigan State**-Trannon 7-93; Scott 5-87; Reed 4-32; Teague 3-3; Ringer 2-(-1); Brown 1-25; Stanton 1-(-6).

Interceptions: **Penn State**-Zemaitis 3-17; Johnson 1-0. **Michigan State**-None.

Sacks (Unassisted-Assisted): **Penn State**-Alford 2-0. Michigan State-None.

Tackles (Unassisted-Assisted): **Penn State**-Connor 9-5; Harrell 6-6; Hali 4-4; Lowry 3-5; Zemaitis 7-0; T. Shaw 4-3; Posluszny 2-3; Kilmer 3-1; Rice 1-3; Phillips 1-3; Team 3-0; Alford 2-1; Johnson 2-0; Paxson 1-1. **Michigan State**-Bazemore 8-0; E. Smith 5-2; Team 6-0; Peko 3-3; Thornhill 5-0; Adams 2-3; Cooper 3-0; Herron 1-1; Ryan 1-1.

OPPOSITE PAGE: **Penn State's Tim Shaw (20) and Dan Connor (40) stop Michigan State's Jehuu Caulcrick (30) in the third quarter. The Nittany Lions' defense frustrated the Spartans' offensive attack all game.**
Craig Houtz/Centre Daily Times

"I think it would be a great feeling no matter what. But coming through what we've come through and being able to come out this season like we did was just the greatest feeling in the world."

—E.Z. Smith, center

The Nittany Lions, as they have for most of the season, didn't seem as though they were forcing much at all. Linebacker Dan Connor led Penn State with 14 tackles and safety Chris Harrell added 12. Hunt had 61 of his 89 rushing yards and a touchdown in the fourth quarter. Deon Butler caught his ninth touchdown of the season, and Ethan Kilmer was again impressive with four special teams tackles.

After surrendering more than 300 yards rushing in a 41-18 loss to Minnesota the week before, the Spartans held Penn State to just 293 total yards of offense.

"They came out and they were solid for the most part," said Michigan State coach John L. Smith of his defenders. "They played against some tough kids. But we just can't afford to turn the ball over like we did, and if we take

that out, we did a good job defending Penn State today."

The Spartans, who lost for the sixth time in seven games, also handcuffed themselves with seven penalties for 55 yards. Kicker Matt Haughey missed a 38-yard field goal, and the Spartans failed to get another field-goal attempt off when holder Fields dropped a snap in the fourth quarter.

The Nittany Lions, on the other hand, were turnover-free until Robinson fumbled at his own 27-yard line with just over two minutes remaining. Stanton hit Kerry Reed for a 15-yard touchdown four plays later and ran in the two-point conversion to account for the game's final margin.

Then the Nittany Lions, so fiercely focused on the game ahead all season, finally allowed themselves to revel in the moment before a sizable Penn State section of the crowd. They decided not to dump water on Paterno, who was fighting a bad

cold, but the 78-year-old coach did say his players offered to take him out on the town that night.

"I've been around a lot of good football teams and I've been in a lot of locker rooms where we've felt pretty good about what we had done," Paterno said. "The kids are the ones that are all fired up and they should be, because they went through all that junk."

Penn State's seniors, who shouldered the burden of 3-9 and 4-7 seasons, will savor a regular season that was one second in Ann Arbor from perfection a little more than their younger teammates.

"I think it would be a great feeling no matter what," said center E.Z. Smith. "But coming through what we've come through and being able to come out this season like we did was just the greatest feeling in the world."

Most preseason predictions, as several Nittany Lions made it a point to remind reporters after the game, had Penn State in the middle of the conference pack. Dreams of a Big Ten title were scoffed at—by everyone but the Nittany Lions, that is. Ignoring their critics and pushing aside their past, they set their goals, worked toward them and let the rest happen on the field until the dream became a reality.

"We believed," Robinson said, "and that's all it takes, is belief."

LEFT: Penn State's Ethan Kilmer recovers his own fumble after catching a pass against Michigan State's Michael Bazemore (40) and Kaleb Thornhill. *Craig Houtz/Centre Daily Times*

Penn State's Ethan Kilmer (34) congratulates Matt Hahn, right, who recovered a blocked punt in the end zone for a touchdown. The score helped the Nittany Lions pull away from the Spartans.
Craig Houtz/Centre Daily Times

Penn State Team Statistics (as of November 20, 2005)

Category	Penn State	Opponent
Scoring	387	181
Points Per Game	35.2	16.5
FIRST DOWNS	238	197
Rushing	125	74
Passing	95	109
Penalties	18	14
RUSHING YARDAGE	2415	1090
Yards Gained Rushing	2656	1460
Yards Lost Rushing	241	370
Rushing Attempts	455	416
Average Per Rush	5.3	2.6
Average Per Game	219.5	99.1
Touchdowns Rushing	27	11
PASSING YARDAGE	2252	2282
Att-Comp-Int	292-154-9	392-222-15
Average Per Pass	7.7	5.8
Average Per Catch	14.6	10.3
Average Per Game	204.7	207.5
Touchdowns Passing	17	10
TOTAL OFFENSE	4667	3372
Total Plays	747	808
Average Per Play	6.2	4.2
Average Per Game	424.3	306.5
KICK RETURNS (NUMBERS-YDS)	25-565	57-1154
PUNT RETURNS (NUMBERS-YDS)	36-396	18-114
INT RETURNS (NUMBERS-YDS)	15-152	9-107
KICK RETURN AVERAGE	22.6	20.2
PUNT RETURN AVERAGE	11.0	6.3
INTERCEPTION RETURN AVERAGE	10.1	11.9
FUMBLES LOST	22-11	15-9
PENALTIES-YARDS	49-379	71-580
Average Per Game	34.5	52.7
PUNTS-YARDS	50-2035	75-3138
Average Per Punt	40.7	41.8
Net Punt Average	38.4	36.6
TIME OF POSSESSION/GAME	29:08	30:52
THIRD-DOWN CONVERSIONS	65/145	68/190
Third-Down Percentage	45%	36%
FOURTH-DOWN CONVERSIONS	6/6	9/17
Fourth-Down Percentage	100%	53%
SACKS BY-YARDS	38-254	11-81
MISCELLANEOUS YARDS	69	23
TOUCHDOWNS SCORED	49	21
FIELD GOALS-ATTEMPTS	15-20	11-19
PAT ATTEMPTS	46-48	14-14
ATTENDANCE (AVERAGE)	104,859	65,820

Score by Quarters

	1st	2nd	3rd	4th	Total
Penn State	75	140	68	104	387
Opponent	23	43	28	87	181

Individual Statistics (as of November 20, 2005)

Rushing

Rushing	GP	Att	Gain	Loss	Net	Avg	TD	Long	Avg/G
Tony Hunt	11	174	1080	33	1047	6.0	6	70	95.2
Michael Robinson	11	146	892	107	785	5.4	11	39	71.4
Justin King	11	17	241	13	228	13.4	0	61	20.7
Austin Scott	10	40	180	17	163	4.1	1	24	16.3
Derrick Williams	7	22	116	11	105	4.8	3	20	15.0
Rodney Kinlaw	7	16	47	13	34	2.1	2	10	4.9
BranDon Snow	11	9	24	1	23	2.6	3	7	2.1
Jordan Norwood	9	1	17	0	17	17.0	0	17	1.9
Nick Pinchek	1	4	15	0	15	3.8	0	6	15.0
Terrell Golden	11	2	15	2	13	6.5	0	15	1.2
Matt Hahn	10	2	12	3	9	4.5	0	12	0.9
Dan Lawlor	3	2	8	0	8	4.0	0	4	2.7
Deon Butler	11	1	6	0	6	6.0	0	6	0.5
Anthony Morelli	6	4	3	11	-8	-2.0	1	2	-1.3
Team	10	15	0	30	-30	-2.0	0	0	-3.0
Total	11	455	2656	241	2415	5.3	27	70	219.5
Opponents	11	416	1460	370	1090	2.6	11	25	99.1

Passing

Passing	GP	Effic	Att-Cmp-Int	Pct	Yds	TD	Long	Avg/G
Michael Robinson	11	129.39	272-141-9	51.8	2097	16	59	190.6
Anthony Morelli	6	146.60	20-13-0	65.0	155	1	55	25.8
Total	11	130.57	292-154-9	52.7	2252	17	59	204.7
Opponents	11	106.30	392-222-15	56.6	2282	10	65	207.5

Receiving

Receiving	GP	No.	Yds	Avg	TD	Long	Avg/G
Deon Butler	11	36	678	18.8	9	54	61.6
Jordan Norwood	9	26	312	12.0	0	31	34.7
Derrick Williams	7	22	289	13.1	1	41	41.3
Tony Hunt	11	19	203	10.7	0	33	18.5
Isaac Smolko	11	11	171	15.5	0	25	15.5
Terrell Golden	11	9	210	23.3	1	56	19.1
Ethan Kilmer	11	9	157	17.4	2	55	14.3
King, Justin	11	5	99	19.8	2	59	9.0
Brendan Perretta	6	5	39	7.8	0	13	6.5
Austin Scott	10	3	27	9.0	0	23	2.7
Lydell Sargeant	8	2	27	13.5	0	23	3.4
Matt Hahn	10	2	19	0	10	9.5	1.9
BranDon Snow	11	2	12	6.0	0	7	1.1
Patrick Hall	10	2	6	3.0	2	3	0.6
Rodney Kinlaw	7	1	3	3.0	0	3	0.4
Total	11	154	2252	14.6	17	59	204.7
Opponents	11	222	2282	10.3	10	65	207.5

Punt Returns

Punt Returns	No.	Yds	Avg	TD	Long
Calvin Lowry	30	335	11.2	0	43
Anthony Scirrotto	5	42	8.4	0	12
Donnie Johnson	1	19	19.0	0	0
Matt Hahn	0	0	0.0	1	0
Total	36	396	11.0	1	43
Opponents	18	114	6.3	0	23

Interceptions

Interceptions	No.	Yds	Avg	TD	Long
Alan Zemaitis	5	17	3.4	0	17
Calvin Lowry	4	36	9.0	0	36
Nolan McCready	71	76	76.0	1	76
Anthony Scirrotto	1	0	0.0	0	0
Chris Harrell	1	16	16.0	0	16
Donnie Johnson	1	0	0.0	0	0
Tony Davis	1	0	0.0	0	0
Anwar Phillips	1	7	7.0	0	7
Total	15	152	10.1	1	76
Opponents	9	107	11.9	0	25

Kick Returns

Kick Returns	No.	Yds	Avg	TD	Long
Derrick Williams	13	274	21.1	0	56
Rodney Kinlaw	6	209	34.8	0	77
Matt Hahn	2	26	13.0	0	20
Justin King	2	21	10.5	0	12
Austin Scott	1	15	15.0	0	15
BranDon Snow	1	20	20.0	0	20
Total	25	565	22.6	0	77
Opponents	57	1154	20.2	0	65

Fumble Returns

Fumble Returns	No.	Yds	Avg	TD	Long
Alan Zemaitis	2	51	25.5	2	35
Dan Connor	1	18	18.0	1	18
Total	3	69	23.0	3	35
Opponents	2	23	11.5	0	15

Scoring

Scoring	TD	FGs	PAT Kick	PAT Rush	PAT Rcv	PAT Pass	DXP	Saf	Points
Kevin Kelly	0	15-20	46-47	1-1	0	0-0	0	0	93
Michael Robinson	11	0-0	0-0	0-0	0	0-0	0	0	66
Deon Butler	9	0-0	0-0	0-0	0	0-0	0	0	54
Tony Hunt	6	0-0	0-0	0-0	0	0-0	0	0	36
Derrick Williams	4	0-0	0-0	0-0	0	0-0	0	0	24
BranDon Snow	3	0-0	0-0	0-0	0	0-0	0	0	18
Patrick Hall	2	0-0	0-0	0-0	0	0-0	0	0	12
Ethan Kilmer	2	0-0	0-0	0-0	0	0-0	0	0	12
Justin King	2	0-0	0-0	0-0	0	0-0	0	0	12
Rodney Kinlaw	2	0-0	0-0	0-0	0	0-0	0	0	12
Alan Zemaitis	2	0-0	0-0	0-0	0	0-0	0	0	12
Anthony Morelli	1	0-0	0-0	0-0	0	0-0	0	0	6
Matt Hahn	1	0-0	0-0	0-0	0	0-0	0	0	6
Nolan McCready	1	0-0	0-0	0-0	0	0-0	0	0	6
Dan Connor	1	0-0	0-0	0-0	0	0-0	0	0	6
Terrell Golden	1	0-0	0-0	0-0	0	0-0	0	0	6
Austin Scott	1	0-0	0-0	0-0	0	0-0	0	0	6
Team	0	0-0	0-1	0-0	0	0-0	0	0	0
Total	49	15-20	46-48	1-1	0	0-0	0	0	387
Opponents	21	11-19	14-14	3-3	1	1-3	0	0	181

Total Offense

Total Offense	G	Plays	Rush	Pass	Total	Avg/G
Michael Robinson	11	418	785	2097	2882	262.0
Tony Hunt	11	174	1047	0	1047	95.2
Justin King	11	17	228	0	228	20.7
Austin Scott	10	40	163	0	163	16.3
Anthony Morelli	6	24	-8	155	147	24.5
Derrick Williams	7	22	105	0	105	15.0
Rodney Kinlaw	7	16	34	0	34	4.9
BranDon Snow	11	9	23	0	23	2.1
Jordan Norwood	9	1	17	0	17	1.9
Nick Pinchek	1	4	15	0	15	15.0
Terrell Golden	11	2	13	0	13	1.2
Matt Hahn	10	2	9	0	9	0.9
Dan Lawlor	3	2	8	0	8	2.7
Deon Butler	11	1	6	0	6	0.5
Team	10	15	-30	0	-30	-3.0
Total	11	747	2415	2252	4667	424.3
Opponents	11	808	1090	2282	3372	306.5

Field Goals

Field Goals	FGM-FGA	Pct	01-19	20-29	30-39	40-49	50-99	Lg	Blkd
Kevin Kelly	15-20	75.0	0-0	9-10	4-6	2-3	0-1	47	0
Total	15-20	75.0	0-0	9-10	4-6	2-3	0-1	47	0
Opponents	11-19	57.9	0-0	4-4	3-5	4-8	0-2	47	0

Punting

Punting	No.	Yds	Avg	Long	TB	FC	I20	Blkd
Jeremy Kapinos	50	2035	40.7	60	5	12	19	0
Total	50	2035	40.7	60	5	12	19	0
Opponents	75	3138	41.8	68	3	17	15	1

All Purpose

All Purpose	G	Rush	Rec	PR	KOR	IR	Tot	Avg/G
Tony Hunt	11	1047	203	0	0	0	1250	113.6
Michael Robinson	11	785	0	0	0	0	785	71.4
Deon Butler	11	6	678	0	0	0	684	62.2
Derrick Williams	7	105	289	0	274	0	668	95.4
Calvin Lowry	11	0	0	335	0	36	371	33.7
Justin King	11	228	99	0	21	0	348	31.6
Jordan Norwood	9	17	312	0	0	0	329	36.6
Rodney Kinlaw	7	34	3	0	209	0	246	35.1
Terrell Golden	11	13	210	0	0	0	223	20.3
Austin Scott	10	163	27	0	15	0	205	20.5
Isaac Smolko	11	0	171	0	0	0	171	15.5
Ethan Kilmer	11	0	157	0	0	0	157	14.3
Nolan McCready	9	0	0	0	0	76	76	8.4
BranDon Snow	11	23	12	0	20	0	55	5.0
Matt Hahn	10	9	19	0	26	0	54	5.4
Anthony Scirrotto	9	0	0	42	0	0	42	4.7
Brendan Perretta	6	0	39	0	0	0	39	6.5
Lydell Sargeant	8	0	27	0	0	0	27	3.4
Donnie Johnson	11	0	0	19	0	0	19	1.7
Alan Zemaitis	11	0	0	0	0	17	17	1.5
Chris Harrell	11	0	0	0	0	16	16	1.5
Nick Pinchek	1	15	0	0	0	0	15	15.0
Dan Lawlor	3	8	0	0	0	0	8	2.7
Anwar Phillips	11	0	0	0	0	7	7	0.6
Patrick Hall	10	0	6	0	0	0	6	0.6
Anthony Morelli	6	-8	0	0	0	0	-8	-1.3
Team	10	-30	0	0	0	0	-30	-3.0
Total	11	2415	2252	396	565	152	5780	525.5
Opponents	11	1090	2282	114	1154	107	4747	431.5

Defensive Statistics (as of November 20, 2005)

Defensive Leaders	GP	Solo	Ast	Total Tackles	TFL-Yds	Sacks-Yds	Int-Yds	BrUp	Fumble Rcv-Yds	FF	Blkd Kick	Saf
Paul Posluszny	11	60	51	111	11.0-38	3.0-21	.	2	.	.	.	.
Chris Harrell	11	48	38	86	2.0-5	.	1-16	4	.	.	.	.
Calvin Lowry	11	45	28	73	1.5-16	1.0-13	4-36	2	.	1	.	.
Tim Shaw	11	43	30	73	6.5-29	4.5-25	.	2	.	2	.	.
Dan Connor	8	33	36	69	3.5-16	1.5-5	.	8	1-18	.	.	.
Tamba Hali	11	25	37	62	17.0-86	11.0-79	.	3	.	1	.	.
Matthew Rice	11	20	33	53	8.0-48	5.0-40	.	3	.	.	.	.
Alan Zemaitis	11	34	13	47	1.5-2	.	5-17	10	2-51	2	.	.
Scott Paxson	11	21	17	38	9.0-30	2.5-9	.	1	1-0	.	.	.
Jay Alford	11	13	20	33	9.0-51	7.0-48	.	2	1-0	.	.	.
Anwar Phillips	11	20	6	26	2.0-3	.	1-7	7	.	.	.	.
Ethan Kilmer	11	17	6	23	.	.	.	.	.	1	.	.
Tyrell Sales	11	9	9	18	2.0-4	.	.	1	.	.	.	.
Paul Cronin	5	10	6	16	0.5-2	0.5-2	.	2	1-0	1	.	.
Spencer Ridenhour	11	6	8	14	.	.	.	.	.	.	.	.
Joe Cianciolo	11	6	6	12	0.5-1	.	.	.	1-0	.	.	.
Justin King	11	9	2	11	.	.	.	2	.	.	.	.
Nolan McCready	9	4	5	9	.	.	1-76	.	.	1	.	.
Josh Gaines	10	5	4	9	0.5-1	.	.	1	.	.	.	.
Darien Hardy	11	4	4	8	.	.	.	.	.	.	.	.
Dontey Brown	7	4	3	7	.	.	.	.	.	.	.	.
Sean Lee	7	2	4	6	.	.	.	.	.	.	.	.
Donnie Johnson	11	4	2	6	.	.	1-0	2	.	1	.	.
Mike Lucian	5	3	2	5	0.5-0	.	.	.	.	.	.	.
A.Q. Shipley	11	2	3	5	2.0-12	2.0-12	.	.	.	.	.	.
Tony Davis	9	4	.	4	.	.	1-0	.	.	.	.	.
JR Zwierzynski	8	2	2	4	.	.	.	.	.	.	.	.
Jim Shaw	7	2	2	4	1.0-2	.	.	1	.	.	.	.
Devin Fentress	1	3	.	3	.	.	.	1	.	.	.	.
Jason Ganter	10	3	.	3	.	.	.	.	1-0	1	.	.
Team	10	3	.	3	1.0-3	.	.	1	.	.	.	.
Andy Kubic	11	.	2	2	.	.	.	.	.	.	.	.
Terrell Golden	11	2	.	1	.	.	.	.	.	.	.	.
E.Z. Smith	8	2	.	2	.	.	.	.	1-0	.	.	.
Kevin Darling	4	1	.	1	.	.	.	.	.	.	.	.
Steve Roach	6	1	.	1	.	.	.	.	.	.	.	.
Levi Brown	11	1	.	1	.	.	.	.	.	.	.	.
Lance Antolick	11	1	.	1	.	.	.	.	.	.	.	.
BranDon Snow	11	1	.	1	.	.	.	.	.	.	.	.
Richard Cheek	4	1	.	1	.	.	.	.	.	.	.	.
Austin Scott	10	1	.	1	.	.	.	.	.	.	.	.
Kevin Kelly	11	1	.	1	.	.	.	.	.	.	.	.
Tony Hunt	11	1	.	1	.	.	.	.	.	.	.	.
Anthony Scirrotto	9	.	.	.	.	.	1-0	.	.	.	.	.
Lee Kuzemchak	2	.	.	.	.	.	.	1	.	.	.	.
Total	11	476	380	856	79-351	38-254	15-152	56	9-69	10	1	.
Opponents	11	455	278	733	54-189	11-81	9-107	43	11-23	12	1	.

CLOCKWISE FROM UPPER LEFT:
Defensive coordinator Tom Bradley celebrates the Nittany Lions' win over Michigan State with senior cornerbacks Anwar Phillips (1) and Alan Zemaitis (21). Quarterback Michael Robinson cheers with the Nittany Lions student section as they look forward to a BCS bowl bid. Penn State student Kartik Patel, 21, shows his Lion Pride. Matthew Rice (55) hugs Alan Zemaitis (21) after Zemaitis intercepted a Drew Stanton pass in the end zone in the first quarter.
Game and celebration photos by Craig Houtz/Centre Daily Times
Fan photo by Jason Malmont/Centre Daily Times

ACKNOWLEDGMENTS

SPORTS STAFF

Ron Bracken

Walt Moody

Jeff Rice

Adam Gearhart

Todd Ceisner

Gordon Brunskill

Cecily Cairns

PHOTOGRAPHY STAFF

Laurie Jones

Craig Houtz

Michelle Klein

Nabil K. Mark

Jason Malmont